THOSE DAYS,

That Promise

Some friendships never fade,
Some promises never die

AAnand Soni

Clever Fox® PUBLISHING
Chennai • Bangalore

CLEVER FOX PUBLISHING
Chennai, India

Published by CLEVER FOX PUBLISHING 2025

ISBN: 978-93-7500-078-5

ACKNOWLEDGEMENTS

To my wife, for letting me hide away and ignore life whenever the book needed me. Thank you for the quiet and the patience.

And to my daughter, the best kind of editor. Your random chapter grabs and nonstop questions about what happens next kept this whole crazy journey fun and pushed the story forward.

Before you begin, pause for a moment.

Close your eyes and go back to your school- the bell ringing, the laughter in the corridor, the endless chatter.

Think of that one class photo- everyone in their teenage years, smiling awkwardly, hairstyles all over the place, and now you can hardly tell who's who.

Remember your gang?

The ones who made even boring days fun?

Hold that picture in your mind.

Now open your eyes.

And meet ours.

Sandeep
Pradeep
Gayatri
Me (Gopal)
Nidhi
Sameer

Sara's Birthday

It was 2025, and the Mehta house looked less like a house and more like a mini banquet hall.

Balloons of every size dangled from the ceiling, a "Happy Birthday Sara" banner was tilted slightly, thanks to uneven tape work, and the smell of fresh pizza was powerful enough to make the yoga ladies forget their calorie counts.

Kids were running around like tiny tornados, parents stood in small circles balancing paper plates full of samosas, cake, and gulab jamuns, and in one corner, the DJ kept pushing the bass like he was testing how much the speakers could handle.

Sara, the star of the evening, was everywhere at once. One minute she was cracking jokes with her friends, the next she had grabbed the microphone from the poor professional host.

"Hello, friends and their parents!" Sara announced, standing on a chair for extra height. "Welcome to my sweet sixteen party. It's my birthday… so I also deserve the mic.

The crowd laughed.

Her mother, clapped and joined in the fun. "Sara, let the host do his job!"

"Mom, trust me," Sara grinned, " I'll return the mic in one piece."

The host, a nervous-looking girl in a shiny blue blazer, tried to smile. "Yes, yes, she is the real star tonight."

Sara continued, "Okay, first game: whoever can finish one full slice of pizza without licking their fingers wins 5 Star from me!"

From the kids' corner came a shout:

"I'm in! And I'll win!"

Another voice:

"No chance, I eat pizza like a pro!"

Her mother shook her head, laughing as she picked up a paper plate. "Sara, you're impossible."

Meanwhile, I stood a little away, leaning against the wall. My smile was quiet, my eyes following Sara as she lit up the room. Every laugh, every joke, every clap seemed to revolve around her.

A neighbour aunty passed by and teased, "Gopal ji, your daughter is running the whole show!"

I nodded, chuckling softly. "That's Sara. She doesn't know how to sit still."

The aunty laughed and moved on. I stayed in my corner, watching, listening, soaking it all in like someone who didn't want to miss a single second.

Sara was in her full element. She bounced from one corner of the room to another, pulling her friends into random games and even dragging shy kids onto the dance floor.

"Come on, don't hide near the food table," she pointed at one boy. "Dance first, samosa later."

The boy groaned. "But I already took two samosas…"

"Then dance double," Sara shot back, and the crowd laughed.

The professional host, now reduced to clapping along, whispered into the mic, "Ladies and gentlemen, I think I have lost my job tonight."

Her mother, laughing, walked over to stop her daughter. "Sara, behave! You're not the host of the party."

Sara grinned. "But Mom, I'm the birthday girl. Everyone came here for me, right?"

From the crowd, one boy shouted, "No, we came for the pizza!"

Sara pointed dramatically at him. "Security! Throw him out immediately."

Even the elders chuckled at her antics.

Her mother joined the games too, taking part in a silly round of musical chairs with the kids.

Meanwhile, I remained in my quiet spot. I wasn't the dancing type. I wasn't the loud-cheering type either. But my eyes never left Sara. Every clap, every squeal, every joke of hers pulled my smile a little wider.

A neighbour aunty walked past and said warmly, "Your Sara has such confidence, Gopal ji. She's the real life of the party."

I nodded with a small chuckle. "That's true."

The aunty moved on, and I went back to watching, storing each moment carefully inside me.

The party was in full swing now. Kids were shrieking over a balloon game, the host was finally allowed to run a quiz, and Sara was still darting across the room like a firecracker.

In one corner, a small group of aunties stood with their plates of samosas and cold drinks, talking in that half-whisper-half-loud tone that always reached the wrong ears.

One of them glanced at Sara, who was now holding the mic again and making everyone clap.

"She's so full of energy," the aunty said, smiling. "Confidence just pours out of her."

Another replied with a laugh, "Haan, but look at Gopal. Calm like a temple bell. Sara hasn't inherited even one DNA strand from him!"

The group giggled. For them, it was a light joke, harmless chatter.

But for me, standing not too far away, it was a sharp pin through my chest.

The smile slipped off my face. My hands froze mid-clap.

No one noticed the change. Everyone else was laughing, cheering, and eating.

I turned my head slightly, trying to mask the sudden heaviness. Then, without drawing attention, I stepped back and quietly walked out of the hall.

I slipped into my bedroom and quietly closed the door.

The sudden silence pressed against my ears.

I sat down on the edge of the bed, my hands resting on my knees. For a moment, I stared at the floor, fighting the weight in my chest. Then the tears came, slow, unwilling, but real.

I whispered to myself, almost like admitting a secret.

"Not even a single strand of DNA… yes, that's how it can be."

Outside, the party roared on, the DJ shouting, kids screaming, plates clattering. Inside, I was alone with the ache that had opened inside him.

After a long pause, I stood, walked to the cupboard, and pulled out an old wooden box from the top shelf.

It was worn, corners chipped but carefully kept. The kind of box that doesn't hold things, it holds lifetimes.

I set the old wooden box on the bed, smiling as memories seemed to float out of it.

For a long moment, I didn't open it.

I just sat there, staring.

The voices from the hall floated faintly through the half-open door, laughter, claps, Sara's voice calling someone to dance.

It all sounded so far away now.

I took a deep breath and lifted the lid.

Inside lay the scattered pieces of another lifetime, some cards, a few papers, old photographs, a T-shirt, and a diary that had somehow survived the years.

Each item had its own story.

Each one was a doorway to a day I thought I'd forgotten.

I hesitated for a moment, afraid to touch anything.

Then my eyes fell on the diary at the bottom, thick, and brown, its edges curled with age.

I picked it up carefully. The cover still read, in bold handwriting:

"Gopal Mehta, Class XII-C, Year 1996."

As I turned the pages, something slipped out from between them, a photograph.

I caught it before it fell.

Not just one face, but a group of them.

A gang of friends, all smiles and chaos.

A laugh escaped me before I even realised it.

"The LLB gang…" I whispered, my voice breaking just a little.

My lips trembled into a smile. I traced each face in the photo with my finger, whispering their names under my breath.

"Piddu…"

"Sandy…"

"Gayatri"

"Me.."

"Nidhi..." and

"Sam..."

And just like that, the past came rushing back. It was 1996 again.

The First Meeting

June 1996, Ahmedabad

It was 8:00 a.m. on a hot June day in Ahmedabad.

Ahmedabad in June was no joke. The sun didn't rise, it attacked. By 8 a.m., the tar roads already looked like they were plotting to melt the soles of my Bata shoes. Rickshaw drivers wiped sweat with gamchas, hawkers shouted at the top of their voice, and the smell of dust mixed with fried fafda floated in the air.

I was travelling in the legendary AMTS bus (Ahmedabad Municipal Transport Service) to my new school, Karnavati Vidyalaya, Shahibaug (KVS).

We had just shifted from Delhi, thanks to my father's *pack-your-bags* transferable government job. It was my first day at KVS. The new term of the school had already started 10 days ago, but between packing, moving, and all the transfer-related chaos, the kind where school admission forms are always the last thing to come out of the suitcase, my admission got delayed.

Every teenage boy, on the edge of stepping into adulthood, wants to look good and presentable on the first day of school, and of course, every day after that too, in case destiny decided to introduce him to his 'future wife' in the corridor.

So last night, I put in full *Filmfare Award* level effort: one hour to iron my white shirt and blue trousers, thirty minutes to shine my black school shoes till they could reflect my future, and another half an hour this morning to comb my hair… with a little gel for that *hero* touch.

According to my mother, my tall, thin frame, fair complexion, brown silky hair, and brown eyes made me a "limited-edition handsome model." According to me, I just hoped I didn't look like a scarecrow who had borrowed a school uniform for the day.

I boarded route number 56, the bus that snakes past a couple of colleges and then down Ashram Road, the corporate jungle where half the city's tie-wearing population clocks in.

The bus was packed tighter than a Mumbai local at rush hour, elbows jabbing, bags hanging in mid-air, and every inch of space already claimed.

Most of the crowd was college students, the kind who turn public transport into their personal entertainment zone. A few were singing so loudly, I wondered if they were auditioning for a national award in *torture-by-music*. Others were cracking jokes and laughing as if their semester results depended on it.

At the door, a bunch of boys hung out dangerously, doing their "roadside Sharukh Khan- DDLJ" act, minus the charm and definitely minus Kajol. They were singing songs with full filmi emotion, and the volume shot up two notches every time a girl walked past.

And then came the "mercy face" brigade, the everyday warriors who didn't want to get up, but had to. They'd hurried through their morning, grabbed their lunch box, and squeezed into this bus, all in the hope of making it to the office before the boss's glare.

People like me, school kids, quiet and lost in thought, were definitely the minority. The bus felt like two teams, the majority (college kids) and the minority (mercy faces + school-goers). The minority had two options, laugh along with the majority or silently judge them with creative facial expressions.

I was standing in the middle of this crowded, dancing bus, dancing not because of music, but thanks to government-sponsored potholes, when I felt a tap on my back. I turned my head slowly, navigating between arms, elbows, and handles hanging from the ceiling.

"Ticket," came the voice.

The voice belonged to a short, round-bellied man with dark skin, a thick moustache, and a week-old stubble. He wore the classic khaki half-sleeved shirt, the unmistakable uniform of a bus conductor in India.

"Student pass," I replied with the pride of a soldier flashing his medal, while very deliberately avoiding eye contact, the classic student trick to avoid small talk or awkward questions about expiry dates.

The conductor didn't like that one bit. His moustache twitched, and he leaned a little closer, as if trying to force my gaze. That silent pause felt longer than the bus ride itself, until he finally tore the ticket stub and moved on with a grunt that clearly said, "Oh! Hero, show me the pass," with a slight glare.

I looked at him as if to say, "Bhai, in this roller-coaster bus, you want me to fish out a pass? Really?" But he repeated, this time with more authority: "Oh! Hero, make it fast."

With all my strength, I managed to take my school bag down from my back, put my right hand into the front pocket, and began digging through the chaos inside. "Come out, hero… your entry scene is here. Don't make me look like the side character in my own story," I urged silently, sifting past pens, scraps of paper, and a half-eaten packet of Parle-G.

No luck. "Where's the damn pass?" I thought. My heart sank.

"Hurry up!" he barked.

"Sorry… Conductor… Sir," I said, and trust me, calling him **Sir** was the hardest part of my morning, "I forgot my pass today." I compassionately replied.

"Sir… huuun…" he said, dragging the word like a tired auto rickshaw climbing an uphill road. His smile was thin, but his eyes did a slow, deliberate scan that screamed, "Beta, ab tu gaya."

"No sorry. No pass, buy ticket," he said, matching my earlier attitude note for note, like he'd just pressed the reverse uno card on me.

I searched my pants pockets, my shirt pocket, and the hidden corners of my bag like a detective on a high-profile case. The main suspect, my wallet, was nowhere to be found.

I looked at him with a face overflowing with emotion, practically screaming for mercy.

"No… no… no… no money? Get off the bus immediately," he said, in the cold, clipped tone usually reserved for Bollywood villains right before the interval.

"Please, sir, I have to reach school on time and this……"

"Get down!" he snapped, already reaching for the bell string to stop the bus.

And then…

'Wait, conductor bhaiya,' came a sweet voice from behind me, the kind I instantly knew didn't belong to a man.

Both of us turned. There she was.

"Bhaiya, how much for a ticket?" she asked, holding out a 10-rupee note.

The conductor glanced at her, then at me, and said, 'Five rupees,' looking like a man who wasn't sure what hurt more, that she had saved me, or that she'd 'bhaiya-zoned' him in front of the entire bus."

He took the note, dabbed his thumb on his tongue like it was a sacred ritual, tore out a ticket, and handed it to me, passing the 5-rupee change back to her.

'Thanks… really, thank you. I… I… forgot my wallet today. I'll return the money tomorrow,' I mumbled in the confused tone of a guy who clearly had no idea what one is supposed to say to a girl the first time they meet.

She smiled back. Fair skin, short brown hair tied with a red hairband, average height, same school uniform as mine. "She must be a KVS student," I thought.

"'No, no, it's alright,' she said softly, but there was a tiny glint in her eyes, the kind that seemed to say, 'Tomorrow? Let's see if you could even find me in this bus.'

I stood quietly after that, looking out of the window. The bus was speeding towards school, until it suddenly stopped at Delhi Darwaja. Outside, a group of policemen and traffic cops were blowing their whistles so furiously you'd think they were trying to empty their lungs for the year in one morning, while blocking traffic from all sides.

Some politician must be coming from the airport,' an old man nearby muttered, his face twisted in irritation as he gave his head a sharp stroke to the left.

"It'll take 20-25 minutes," another replied.

"Twenty-five minutes? God, not today," I folded my hands and prayed silently. My first day, and I was already imagining myself walking into school mid-assembly.

I glanced sideways and caught the KVS girl watching me. I quickly unfolded my hands and shoved them into my pockets like nothing happened.

Finally, after a painfully long wait, the siren of a police car blared. One after another, the cars rolled in, I counted them like a cricket score, one, two, three, four….., ten, eleven……, twenty-one twenty-two…… Twenty-three in total.

"Twenty-three cars for one person. And here I am begging for a 5-rupee ticket," I thought. "That's democracy for you."

The bus moved again, and in exactly 10 minutes, we reached the Police Commissioner bus stop, the one closest to KVS.

Students jumped off and ran towards school.

"Oh no… only five minutes to assembly," I muttered, checking my watch like it might have magically add extra minutes if I stared hard enough."

By the time I moved, I was the last KVS student left in the bus. The driver started to pull away, so I literally jumped out and sprinted after the others, trying to guess the way.

And So, It Began...

Karnavati Vidyalaya, Sahi Baugh, I read from far, while rushing to the school, the name written in bold blue letters on the larger arch-shaped board at the main gate.

By the time I reached school, the drums were already beating for assembly. "Oh fish.. assembly is already started" I said, I bent and held my knees with hands and tried to inhale as much as oxygen as fast as a vacuum cleaner.

Now I knew what was that siren sound that I heard while running, which was exactly similar to what I heard at the time of red-carpet arrival of the politician, that was an alert of starting the morning assembly.

I looked left, then right. To my surprise, there were about a dozen students already parked in the late-comer line. For a moment, my heart did a little somersault, relief mixed with embarrassment.

The AMTS girl stood there too, as if destiny was politely reminding me: "*Hero, your grand entry in this school starts in the late-comers line.*"

"Late comers, stand in a straight line!" a student announced, in a tone so serious you'd think he was controlling prisoners of war.

"What a start of first day in the school, ...late comer" I cursed myself silently

Everyone moved and formed a single line, I noticed that AMTS girl was standing right ahead of me.

I looked around, school campus was huge, big 5 storey building with white and blue paint on the external wall, big parking area, one small playing areas, might be for students of first to third standard and a big playing ground which was bit far but I could see students standing in straight lines. I could hear the voice of instruction given by someone over the mike for the proceeding of the assembly but could not see the stage, as it was behind the one portion of the building at the end.

Soon we heard the prayer sung in a chorus along with the music, I folded my hands and closed my eyes to pray.

I opened my eyes once the prayer got over, I felt some relief. I could hear the announcement going on over the mike but failed to understand them as the voice wasn't clear.

I leaned a little closer and whispered, *"What would be next?"* almost in the AMTS girl's ear, like a lost tourist asking for directions in his own city.

"Sorry…!" she blurted, spinning around in a nanosecond, as if I'd asked for her ATM PIN instead of just a reply.

"I said……What would be the next" I whispered again.

"First time came late to school...huun?" she said, smiling like a judge who knew the accused was lying through his teeth.

"Yes," I answered, sounded normal enough. But then I fumbled, "hunn… infact… first day… in this school," my tone dropped like a radio running out of battery.

"First day..? newcomer? " she said "and tagged late comer" she giggled, girls never let a golden chance for leg-pulling go waste.

"Yaa…" I said, nodding slowly, eyes fixed on the ground. My foot found a tiny stone, which I kicked it gently, watching it rolls away.

"Which class?" she whispered, bending down just enough to make it feel like we were plotting some late-comers' conspiracy.

"XII-C" I replied.

"Hey..!" she said, almost jumping in surprise. "Same class!" Her tone had shifted from judge to teammate in less than a minute.

"Shuuuuuuu… silence!" ordered the student monitor, dragging the 'shuu' like a local train whistle.

By that time the assembly was over, and students started marching in a straight line towards their classrooms, the kind of discipline you usually only see in ants marching after a sugar trail, all in rhythm with the instrumental tune of *"Sare Jahaan Se Accha."*

"What happened, students?" I suddenly heard, the voice polite yet commanding, echoed from a little away. I turned my head, praying it wasn't the principal, but curious enough to look anyway.

I saw a man, hardly five feet tall, with an average build and bright red hair, clearly a proud user of mehendi as hair dye. He walked towards us in black trousers, and a brown checked half-sleeve shirt, untucked of course, paired with black shoes.

"He is Yadav sir, Geography teacher" She whispered.

"huun.." I nodded

"What happened students" he repeats again, once he came close to us.

His lips were bright red, clearly stained by *paan*, which, I guessed, he must have chewed just before the assembly.

"Sir, let me explain," the AMTS girl replied, taking full charge on behalf of all of us late-comers, just like those suiting brand commercials where the model suddenly transforms into a confident hero the moment he slips into the blazer.

For the next few minutes, she confidently narrated the entire episode of the morning car parade, the very reason all of us had ended up late.

I was busy watching Yadav Sir's face, his expressions kept changing with every sentence she spoke, like he was silently rating her story out of ten.

"Okay… I'll give you all the benefit of doubt. Sunit, note down their names and let them go," he said. Yadav Sir walked off towards the main gate, his red hair catching the sun, leaving behind a trail of paan-flavoured authority.

"Benefit of doubt..? Wah, thank you Mr. Harsha Bhogle," I chuckled inside, smiling as if I had just survived an LBW appeal.

"Come let's hurry up" She said, "Our first period would be of Sharma sir...accountancy, he is our class teacher also".

We started walking, almost breaking into a run, towards the main entrance of the building.

"By the way, my name is Gayatri," she said, stretching out her right hand for a handshake. A yellow band dangled from her wrist, which looked like a friendship band,

"Gayatri... such a divine name," I thought, staring at her for a second. *Her family must be the type who never miss their temple visit.*

"What.?" she said.

"Nothing," I said with a quick shake of my head. "I'm Gopal." I extended my right hand, and we shook hands, the first handshake of my new school life.

"Gopal... such a divine name," she mumbled, glancing the other way. *Her family must be very spiritual,* I heard her whisper under her breath. I almost laughed inside, the exact same thought I'd had when I first heard her name, *Gayatri.*

"What.?" I asked.

"Nothing" She replied.

"Strange... two strangers, same thought, same class, same late-comer line. Maybe this was how friendship was meant to begin." I thought and smiled.

"My friends call me GEM," I told her.

"Gem...?" she said, dragging it out with a raised brow. "How come?"

"My full name is Gopal Easwar Mehta," I said with a smile. "So naturally... GEM." I shrugged, as if it was the most obvious thing in the world.

We arrived at the end of the ground-floor corridor. "Arrived, Class XII C," she announced, pointing towards the tiny board above the closed door, like a tour guide ending her morning shift.

The door was closed. "Sir has come," she said, then paused, taking a deep breath before slowly letting the air out through her lips.

She pushed the door gently with both hands, bent forward slightly, and said softly, "Good morning, Sir, may I…" She paused, turned her eyes towards me, and corrected herself: "Can we come in?"

"Please come. Gayatri" a firm voice called from inside.

She entered the classroom, "Come" she looked back and said. I stepped in after her.

"Yes?" Sharma sir looked up.

"Good morning, sir....my name is Gopal Mehta, I came from......" before I could finish, he said with his voice rising, "Oh Gopal….I know….I know.... please come".

He half-sat on the table, balancing on his left side, and placed his left hand on my back. The gesture was oddly comforting, like a coach encouraging a first-time player before the match begins.

I could feel a dozen eyes scanning me from top to bottom, the kind of silent inspection only classmates can do.

"Late-comer on the first day itself… haan?" he chuckled. A low ripple of laughter passed through the classroom, just loud enough to turn my ears warm

"Oh God… not again," I muttered to myself, annoyed. Yet my eyes didn't budge from Sharma Sir.

"Students, Gopal is a new student in our classroom. I welcome him on behalf of all of us," Sharma Sir said, raising his voice a little louder. He placed his hand on my right shoulder and gently turned me towards the class.

"His father got transferred from Delhi" he added. I took a quick glance of every one's face and looked for a second at Gayatri, smiled.

"Where will you sit…?" he muttered, glancing thoughtfully across the boys' benches like a chess player planning his next move.

"Sirji how would I know" I thought.

"Where is Nitin today?" he asked, pointing at one empty seat.

"He is on medical leave, Sir, for 3 days," one boy replied.

"Gopal, please sit there till Nitin resume, will rearrange sitting arrangement soon" he said and patted my back.

He pointed to the left corner seat, third bench, third row.

I observed the class was having four lanes with five rows each and first two rows were for girls, and next three rows were of boys. I have to sit on the seat from where the boy's section was beginning.

From the corner of my eye, I noticed that Gayatri was sitting on the adjacent bench, the last in the girl's row.

"Thank you, sir," I said, and I obeyed the order.

Sharma sir begun his class and everyone were patiently listing what he was saying.

And just like that, my first day as a newcomer had begun.

The First Chapter of Friendship

"Finally, the first day was over. Except for the morning chain of shockers, it went well," I was thinking while waiting for the AMTS bus at the Police commissioner bus stop.

I noticed Gayatri walking towards the stop, a little spring in her step in her step. Both hands clutched her bag straps tightly, as if the bag carried top-secret files instead of notebooks.

I guessed she was going to board the same bus, after all, she had come in the same one that morning. But I acted like I hadn't noticed her at all. But instead of looking at her, I turned my head dramatically towards the other side of the road.

"Hey Gopal...!" she called out and smiled.

"Hi! Gayatri" I replied and smiled back.

"How was your first day? Good, haan? Did you like the students and teachers here?" she asked, firing questions faster than the morning bus conductor shouting "Ticket! Ticket!"

"Pause....pause... lady" I screamed *inside my head.*

"Great..." I said out loud, pausing mid-sentence because i had no clue what to say next.

"Chocolate?" she pulled out two small five-star bars from her pocket and offered me one.

"No thank you" I replied.

"Don't be so formal, Gopal, take it" she said, tearing open one bar. "Tomorrow, you buy for me," she giggled, taking a bite.

"Thanks" I said, accepting mine, tearing the wrapper, and taking a small bite.

We stood quietly for few minutes.

Route No. 56 RTO circle to Shyamal char rasta, I read on the top of the bus.

Hands shot up in the air to stop the bus. Honestly, for us Indians, that gesture is coded in our DNA, you'll find uncles raising their hands at trains too, as if the driver might stop just for them.

"Will you catch this one?" She asked.

"Yes" I said.

The bus stopped and climbed aboard. Being afternoon, it wasn't crowed.

I saw Gayatri had already taken a window seat. I hesitated for a second, if i should sit beside her, and started scanning for another seat.

"Come sit" she said, patted her hand on the empty seat adjacent to her.

"Thanks" I said, I sat down and took my bag from my right solder and kept on my lap.

"Are you like this always or just trying to impress me?" she giggled,

"Again, lady..." I thought.

"You will know gradually," I said, pretending it was some deep philosophical line, when, in truth, my brain was completely blank.

"Anyways.. Gopal tell me about you" she said, neatly folding the chocolate wrapper and slipping it into her skirt pocket.

"My father works as an officer in the Income Tax Department, my mother is a housewife, and I'm the only son. Our roots are in Ahmedabad, but thanks to my father's transferable job, I was born in Mumbai and spent quite a few years there. Then we moved to Delhi, and now we're back in Ahmedabad," I stopped, as if waiting for applause.

"Great," she said. "So, you're a Gujju?" Trust us Indians to shorten everything even a perfectly decent word like Gurujati becomes Gujju.

"Yes, and you?" I asked, tossing the question back like a rapid-fire round.

"I am a Punjabi" she said.

"I've never really heard the name Gayatri among Punjabis," I said curious, like I'd just seen butter chicken served with khichdi.

She looked at me for a few seconds, then said, "My mother is Hindu," and smiled, as if that explained everything in a single line.

A few minutes passed in silence. The bus crawled past Delhi Darwaja Crossroad, the same traffic trap we'd been struck in that morning.

She broke the silence. "Where do you stay, Gopal?" She asked.

"Shyamal Char Rasta" I replied.

"Great…..Me too." She said louder than normal one. I looked at people around us.

"Thand rakh lady" I murmured to myself, wondering why she got so excited every time she heard something that connected back to her.

The conductor arrived and repeated his trademark line, "Ticket?" Before I could start my student-pass speech, she slipped out a five-rupee note and paid for my ticket as if it were the easiest thing in the world. I just sat there, quietly smiling, sometimes, kindness comes wrapped in the smallest things.

"Where in Shyamal char rasta? I mean..in which Society" She asked, "I stay in Elegance". Then she turned towards me, eyes full of curiosity.

"I stay in Sky-view" I replied.

"Next to couple of society near to my society" she said.

I nodded politely, even though I had no clue where her society actually was.

For next half an hour or so she talked about Ahmedabad food joints, place for hangouts, from where to do shopping and all the things which a person should know who is new to this city, a free city guide.

"Destination has come" she said,

I looked up. "So quick?" I thought.

We got down from the bus.

We started walking towards our society. My society was around 10 minutes' walk away from the bus stop.

"Do you have any friends here?" she asked.

"No… don't know anyone here right now," I paused, then added quickly, "except you."

She burst out laughing, louder than I expected.

"You can call me GEM—Gayatri," she said, trying to sound cool, though my voice probably wobbled like a loose ceiling fan

"Oh..! GEM… yaa, yaa… but your *friends* call you GEM, right?" she teased, giggling.

"Friends?" I asked, raising my right hand to shake.

"Friends," she said, clasping my hand.

"Bye…GEM" she said as her society came.

"Bye" I replied. I walked towards my society.

— Friendship Became a Bond —

It had been a little over two weeks since I joined the new school. The classroom full of identical uniforms was slowly revealing who was who. Some loud, some quiet, some always raising their hands like they were on a quiz show.

But if I had to be honest, the only classmate I really knew well was Gayatri. She and I shared the same bus every morning and evening. She was the outspoken, talkative one, always finding something to say, while I tried to stay as quiet as possible. And maybe that's how the friendship began, one talking, the other listening, slowly finding a rhythm that worked.

It was a normal Tuesday morning, but the geography teacher walked into the classroom with a big smile.

There was something unique about him, half his hair dyed orange with mehendi, a half-sleeved shirt left untucked, and a pair of spotless white shoes. Every time I looked at him, I wondered from which angle I was supposed to call him "Sir," and that too a geography sir.

"Class," he announced, writing on the blackboard in his best cursive, "Group Project: Save Environment."

There was something unique about his handwriting too. Between the "G" and the "t," the letters would slope at nearly a forty-five degree angle. To read it, you had to literally tilt your head, first decode the artistic curves, and only then figure out what was actually written.

"The best project will be nominated for the inter-school 'Save Environment' competition," he said, drawing a long line under the topic on the board.

Immediately, a boy from the back muttered, "Do we have any option to skip it?" Everyone giggled.

"Oh yes, one more thing," he added, adjusting his spectacles, "this will carry a weightage of five percent in your final geography practical exam for the board." He paused.

"Oh, and someone here was saying something about skipping this?" he asked, with a sarcastic smile.

"No..No sir, it's a brilliant idea, Yadav Sir," one boy muttered with all seriousness. The class laughed.

"Form groups of five or six now. Someone help me note down the group names along with the students," he said firmly, putting the chalk down as if to close the matter.

That was it. Chaos exploded.

Everyone rushed to grab their best friends, and within minutes the classroom looked less like a project discussion and more like an IPL auction.

The very first groups to form, within seconds, were the ones made up of all the studious kids, or at least the ones who pretended to be.

"First benchers all with me, okay?" one of the studious types declared, as if she was distributing government quotas.

In a few minutes, almost the entire class had split into different groups. Some students looked thrilled because they had managed to stick with their closest friends. A few others weren't so lucky, their so-called friends had ditched them at the last moment and happily jumped into another group, leaving behind long faces and silent sulks.

Amid all the chaos, Gopal stood quietly near his bench. He wasn't the kind to shout or run. Clutching his notebook, he looked around, trying to figure out which group to join. He did attempt to move towards a couple of groups, but before he could even take a step, those groups had already sealed themselves shut.

"Bro, our group is full," someone said when he tried to move closer. Another group laughed, "Sorry yaar, we're already six."

For a teenager, that "sorry" hurt more than a Chauhan sir's scolding.

The classroom buzzed with energy, but for Gopal, it felt silent. Everyone had their group. He didn't.

At that moment, Gayatri noticed him. She was sitting with two friends already, busy deciding roles.

Gayatri looked up, saw Gopal standing awkwardly near the back, pretending to read his notebook. Something about that sight made her raise her hand.

"Gopal!" she called out, smiling.

He looked around, unsure. "Me?"

"Yes, you! Come here. Join our group."

A few heads turned. One boy whispered, "Arrey Gayatri, we are already five?"

She shrugged, "So what? we can add one more as per Yadav sir" and patted the empty space on the bench beside her.

"Yes, no worries," a girl whispered from the group, and the others quickly nodded in agreement.

Gopal walked slowly, still hesitant, but sat down. His relief was visible.

"A quick introduction, Gopal, this is Saurabh, that's Amit, she's Pooja, and she's Nidhi," she rattled off in less than two seconds.

I smiled and gave a small nod, the kind you give when you've already forgotten half the names.

"So, what would be our theme for the project" Gayatri asked to the group. She had already elected herself as the lead of the group.

Someone suggested, "Let's make a windmill model."

Another quickly added, "No, no, a solar plant model will be better."

Then Gayatri jumped in, her voice full of energy. "How about a model of a whole village? With nature, animals, a river, mountains, everything in one place!" She spoke with such passion, waving her hands in the air, each gesture perfectly in sync with her words.

"Wow, yes, yes, brilliant idea!" almost everyone echoed together, their voices overlapping in excitement.

As the group debated, Gopal didn't speak yet, but the smile on his face said enough. In a class full of noise, one person had noticed him.

A seed of friendship had been planted. Yadav sir clapped his hands to settle everyone. "Alright, I hope all groups are ready. Remember, this is about teamwork and you need to submit the project before the weekend, so all the best."

"Cardboard, thermocol, paints," Nidhi quickly listed down the items, as if the teacher had asked for roll call, all while trying to figure out the approximate budget needed for the project.

"How much will it cost?" another asked.

"Around fifty rupees per person," Nidhi replied.

For school students in the 90s, fifty rupees wasn't exactly pocket change. It meant giving up samosas and Fanta bottles for at least a week. But the cheer of the group drowned out such worries.

"Yes, yes, we'll all contribute."

"It will look amazing, like a real village."

"We'll win the competition for sure!"

Plans were flying faster than kites on Uttarayan. Who would bring what, which shop had the best thermocol, who could draw mountains that didn't look like potato chips, everything was being debated with full energy.

In the middle of this cheerful noise, Gopal sat quietly. He wasn't against the idea, but he kept thinking about the cost, the waste, the effort. Finally, in a small voice, he spoke up.

"Why don't we try posters, slogans, and drawings instead? Less cost, more impact. Easy to explain also."

The group froze for half a second, then burst out laughing.

"Posters?" one boy smirked.

"What are we, nursery kids?" another teased.

"The jury will throw us out if we take that," someone else added.

Even those who didn't laugh outright smiled politely, the way people do when a relative cracks a bad joke at dinner.

I felt my cheeks warm. I looked down at the notebook, pretending to adjust the pen. I didn't argue further.

Gayatri, though, had noticed. She saw the way my shoulders dropped when they dismissed my idea, the way I avoided eye contact, the way I folded my notebook like it had suddenly become very interesting.

She didn't say anything right then. The group was still buzzing, too caught up in their cardboard dreams. But she tucked away the thought in her mind. Gopal wasn't lazy, he wasn't clueless. He had a point, maybe even a better one, but it wasn't loud enough to win a majority, not even a single vote.

The discussion continued late into the period, with everyone arguing about colours and shapes as if they were designing the next housing colony. I scribbled quietly on the edge of the page, sketching a tree, a river, a few stick figures holding banners. Nobody noticed.

What I didn't know was that Gayatri had noticed everything.

Once the group had agreed on the cardboard village idea, the next step was obvious, money. The moment Nidhi opened her notebook to note contributions, it felt less like a classroom project and more like a mini income-tax collection drive.

"Fifty rupees each," she announced with authority, holding out her pencil box as if it were a donation box. One by one, students pulled out crumpled notes from pencil pouches, shirt pockets, and between pages of textbooks where money was usually hidden.

"Here's mine."

"Add my name."

"Count properly, Nidhi, don't eat our money!" someone teased.

Nidhi rolled her eyes but kept writing, "Saurabh – 50, Amit – 50, Pooja – 50…"

When it came to my turn, I hesitated. I fiddled with my notebook before speaking softly.

"I'll bring it tomorrow."

A couple of heads turned.

Nidhi raised her eyebrow. "Okay… but don't forget."

I nodded quickly, avoiding eye contact. My voice was almost lost in the classroom noise.

Then, as the group began discussing materials, I tried again.

"Maybe posters and drawings would work better. We can make slogans… more awareness, less waste."

This time, no one even bothered to laugh.

"Arrey yaar, not again," Amit groaned.

"Forget posters. The village model will look amazing."

"The jury doesn't want drawings, they want models," Pooja declared with finality.

It was settled. My idea was dismissed, neatly folded away like an old homework sheet nobody checked. I went silent again.

Gayatri noticed. She always did. She caught the way my shoulders dropped, the way I tapped my pen nervously, the way my "tomorrow" sounded less about money and more about something else.

When the last round of contributions came, she quietly slipped in an extra note.

"This is for me and Gopal, will take it from him," she said casually. Nobody questioned. Everyone was too busy planning who would buy what.

I glanced at her, confused. She didn't say anything, just gave a small smile, as if telling me not to worry.

The group moved on, buzzing with energy, talking about paints, thermocol sheets, and how to carry everything without breaking it. But I kept thinking about it. My idea hadn't found a place, my money hadn't gone in, but someone had still made sure I wasn't left out.

The entire day went by in endless discussions and planning for the project. Everyone in the group was buzzing with excitement, tossing around ideas and tasks like cricket balls at practice.

We were walking towards the bus stop. The road was noisy with honking scooters and street vendors shouting about peanuts and guavas. Amid all that noise, I was unusually quiet, quieter than my usual quiet self.

"Why are you so against the model, Gopal? You're an artist. You should be excited."

I shifted the bag on my shoulder, eyes fixed on the road. "It's not the model," I said slowly. "I just feel we need a smarter way, something that gives a quick but wonderful result. We only have two or three days left, that's it."

"Hmmm," Gayatri replied, her tone not fully convincing.

The bus arrived with its usual screech, and passengers pushed their way in. Gayatri and I slipped into our usual spot, the last row, near the window. She took the window seat, as always.

For the next few minutes, there was silence. But it was the kind of silence that isn't empty. I could sense Gayatri wanted to say something, only she was waiting for the right trigger to begin.

She opened her mouth a couple of times to say something, but each time she stopped midway. I could sense a bit of discomfort in her, like she wanted to ask me something but wasn't sure how to ask.

"Gayatri, listen," I finally said. "It's not the model." The words came out slowly, almost as if they hurt on the way out. "It's… the fifty rupees." I couldn't bring myself to look into her eyes, so I kept mine fixed on the moving traffic outside the bus.

Gayatri frowned. "Fifty rupees?"

I didn't say anything, but my face spoke louder than my words. I just kept my eyes fixed on the world outside the window.

Gayatri realised the awkwardness I must have been feeling. She quietly turned her face towards the window, giving me space.

The bus slowed down and halted at the red signal near Income Tax Char Rasta.

"Gopal…" she said softly, almost hesitant, "is there something you want to share?"

I took a deep breath before speaking again. The words felt heavier than they should, but they needed to come out.

"I'm telling you this because I trust you," I said quietly, "but promise me it will stay between us. I don't want others making fun of it."

"My father works as a junior officer in the income tax office. The pay is average, enough to run the house, but not enough when extra troubles pile up. My mother is the only child of her parents, and they live in Ahmedabad. Both of them have been unwell for a long time, and a lot of money has been going into their treatment. Papa even had to take a loan from his PPF account just to manage."

I paused, staring at the blur of scooters rushing past the bus window.

"Last month, my Nani passed away. Nana is alone now, and his health isn't good either. That's why Papa asked for a transfer to Ahmedabad, so we could take care of him. But even his medicines and hospital visits add more expenses. Every month feels heavier than the last."

My voice dropped lower. "So, when everyone started talking about fifty rupees… I just didn't know how to ask for it at home. I knew it would pinch."

Gayatri stayed quiet. Not the kind of silence that feels heavy, but the kind that listens. She didn't rush in with pity or soft words. She just let me speak.

"I thought posters and drawings would be cheaper," I continued, embarrassed, "and maybe better too. But no one wanted that. So…" I shrugged, like the matter was closed.

Gayatri looked at me for a moment, then smiled gently. "You know… not every good idea gets heard the first time. And about the fifty rupees, don't worry".

"You're still part of this group," she added with a small smile and a playful wink.

There was no drama in her tone, no 'bechara' look, no lecture. Just calm support, simple and steady, the kind that didn't make me feel small.

For the next few minutes, Gayatri kept talking. She cracked small jokes, pointed at random things outside the window, and made sure the silence didn't return. It was her way of making sure I didn't feel embarrassed. She went on and on, light and cheerful, right until the bus finally reached our stop and we got down and headed home.

The next two days were nothing short of chaos. Every corner of the classroom turned into a mini workshop. Thermocol, glue, chart papers, and sketch pens were scattered everywhere like exam chits after invigilation.

Each group had its own grand vision. One was building a giant solar plant, complete with shiny foil panels that kept falling off every hour.

Another was attempting a water wheel, which looked more like a broken ceiling fan than a source of energy. The studious group had neatly stacked charts with twenty bullet points each, impressive at first sight, but boring enough to put even the teacher to sleep.

Our group, meanwhile, soldiered on with the cardboard village. Huts went up crooked, the river looked suspiciously like a strip of blue chart paper hurriedly glued in, and the mountains glittered like wedding invitations gone wrong.

By the evening of the second day, the "so-called village" stood complete. It was far from perfect, the huts leaned like tired old men, the pond resembled a giant water stain, and the glitter refused to stay in place, making the whole thing sparkle unintentionally.

We knew it wasn't going to win a contest, but at least it wouldn't collapse before reaching the teacher's table. And in a project like this, that counted as success.

The big day finally arrived. The classroom looked like a noisy exhibition hall, every group proudly carrying their creations like they were moving the Kohinoor diamond. Solar plants with shiny foils, water wheels that refused to spin, posters hanging like election banners, the room was alive with colour, glue stains, and nervous energy.

Our turn came. We carried the cardboard village carefully, like a bride being taken to the mandap. Everything was going fine until tragedy struck and of course, it had to be Amit.

While placing the model on the exhibition table, he slipped on a patch of spilled Fevicol. In one glorious moment, both Amit and the village went down together. The huts crumbled, the pond cracked open, and the mountains flattened like they had just survived a major earthquake.

The room went silent for a moment, then everyone burst out laughing.

"Our eco-friendly village has just faced a natural disaster," someone joked.

"Looks more like post-earthquake rehabilitation now," another added.

We stood frozen, staring at the ruins. The model that had taken two chaotic days to build was now a broken mess, glitter still twinkling on the floor like cruel mockery.

That's when I moved. Without saying a word, I rushed to the help desk near the stage, grabbed a few chart papers and colours, and sat down on the floor. In quick strokes, my hands flew across the paper, sketching a village scene, tall trees, clean rivers, animals grazing, farmers working in harmony. Within minutes, I created drawings that not only matched the broken model but actually made it look like a planned theme.

The damaged huts were now "after-storm survivors," with banners on the charts explaining the importance of rebuilding sustainably. The cracked pond was turned into a "before and after" drawing, showing how water resources could be restored. Even the flattened mountains were paired with a chart that read, *"Nature can destroy, but it can also heal."*

By the time the teacher walked over, our so-called ruined village had transformed into a creative mix of model and artwork. What looked like a disaster was now presented as a "dual-format project", part model, part illustrated story.

The teacher examined everything carefully, tapping her pen against the charts. She finally smiled and said, "This is clever. Anyone can make a model, but this shows real creativity."

The class, which had been snickering a few minutes ago, went quiet. Heads turned towards me. For the first time, no one was laughing at me. They were impressed.

I kept my eyes down, pretending to check the brushes, but everyone could see the faint smile tugging at my lips. And when I finally looked up, my eyes met Gayatri's. She just gave me a small nod, a smile that said, *"See, I told you your work matters."*

For the rest of the day, we moved from one table to another, checking out projects and cracking jokes. The whole day was filled with fun and laughter.

The school day finally ended.

At the bus stop, I walked beside Gayatri.

"Thank you…" I said quietly, breaking the silence. "For everything."

Gayatri looked at me with a grin. "Next time, just do me one favour."

"What?" I asked.

"And don't forget to draw me taller also, at least once in my life."

We both burst out laughing, the kind of laugh that makes people turn around and smile without knowing why.

The bus arrived, and as we climbed in, it felt like something had shifted. A project had been made, marks would be given, but more than that, a friendship had been cemented not with glue or glitter, but with small moments of trust, support, and quiet understanding.

"That day, we didn't just build a project. We built a bond that would last far longer than any chart or model."

My Gang Induction

It's been a few weeks in the new school.

After Nitin returned from his sick leave, I got promoted (or maybe demoted, depending on how you see it) to the corner seat on the second lane, fourth bench... the kind of seat where you're half visible to the teacher and fully visible to trouble.

By now, I had discovered the legend of Class XII-C, 1996 batch, apparently one of the most notorious batches our school had ever produced. And the Oscar for all this mischief clearly went to the **'LLB gang'**, not lawyers in the making, but the self-proclaimed *Lords of the Last Benches.*

Of course, everyone in the class added a spoonful of masala to the chaos, but a few were like the official brand ambassadors of trouble, Sandeep (Sandy), Pradeep (Piddu) and Sameer (Sam). For them, rules were less like boundaries and more like chalk lines on the ground, easy to rub off and redraw.

Sandeep, or *Sandy*, had a body that made every shirt look too small. His cheeks were always round, like he'd just finished lunch. His belt was always under pressure, and his trousers looked like they'd given up long ago. His father was in the Army, but Sandy's battles were with samosas and running in PT. Still, he walked with full confidence, smiling, joking, and somehow always turning every moment, even a scolding, into laughter.

He was short-tempered and brutally blunt. His words had no filter, like a pressure cooker without a whistle, always ready to explode and scare everyone in a five-foot radius.

Pradeep, lovingly called *Piddu*, also known as the 'Red Panther'. *You'll find out how he earned that name a little later*, also came from an Army background. His curly hair looked like it had its own network always active, never in control. Unlike Sandy, he was thin, of average height, and had a wheatish complexion, the kind of look that neither made him stand out nor disappear, just perfectly 'middle seat in the bus' type. But what really made him popular was his sense of humour. With Piddu around, even the dullest economics lecture could feel like a stand-up comedy show, only difference, the ticket price was your tiffin without your permission.

Sameer, better known as *Sam,* not the American one, but our very own desi version, was at least 3–4 years older than the rest of us. Thanks to his glorious track record of repeating Class 6, Class 9, and Class 11, he had practically earned a long-service medal in school. But age had its perks: while we were still learning how to sharpen pencils properly, Sam had already mastered the art of *jugaad.* Need extra chalk? A proxy signature? Or even samosas smuggled in from outside the school gate? Sam's network ran deeper than the telephone exchange.

And there I was, sharing seats with the LLB gang. Though for the record, I was an unwilling neighbour, not an inducted partner in crime. My benchmate was Piddu, while right behind me, in the last row, Sandy sat sharing a bench with Sam.

It was the last period before lunch, our beloved Sports period. The boys were sweating it out on the football ground, chasing the ball like it was the last cold drink left in the canteen fridge, while the girls were busy with an intense game of kho-kho. The boys were charging across the ground, chasing the ball with all their might. Of course, we didn't have fancy football studs, this was Karnavati Vidyalaya, not Brazil. We played in our regular black school shoes, the ones meant for morning assembly, not muddy slide tackles. Within ten minutes, those shiny blacks had proudly transformed into dust-coated browns.

And our crisp white shirts, after one good fall on the ground, which is very usual one, they didn't look white anymore. By the end of the match, the entire team looked less like students of Class XII-C and more like survivors of a dust storm. And the best part? In that grand, dusty appearance, we had to spend the entire second half of school, pretending nothing was wrong with our uniforms.

Now, everyone knew Sandy was strictly allergic to any form of physical activity. For him, Sports period meant 'sitting under the tree and observing life.' Usually, one or the other member of the LLB gang would give him company in his noble mission of avoiding exercise.

That day, the sun was merciless. The thermometer proudly touched 42 degrees, and the air was so dry and heavy it felt like even our sweat had given up. We split into two football teams, which was never an easy job. Out of about 40 students, 15 were girls (busy with their kho-kho game), and a few boys cleverly escaped by declaring sudden injuries. That left us with 20, 10 on each side.

The KVS ground was massive, the kind where 20 kids looked like tiny dots scattered on a desert. Covering that much space was less like playing football and more like doing a never-ending marathon. By the time someone chased the ball to one end, half the team was already out of breath, and the ball itself looked like it was mocking us on its way to the opponent's goal post.

After about fifteen minutes the ground felt like a tandoor, and I was the naan inside. The heat drained me completely. My water bottle was of no use now, it felt like I was sipping steam. Dizzy spells started circling my head.

"Gopal, pass!" Nitin screamed from the front.

But my body had other plans. The dizziness won. Instead of kicking, I trapped the ball under my foot, bent down, and actually picked it up with my hands. "Time please," I panted, huffing like a pressure cooker about to whistle.

"What the hell, Gopal!" Nitin shouted, his voice echoing across the field. He wasn't just angry that I ignored his golden pass; he was fuming because by touching the ball with my hands, I had basically killed his dream goal. From his face, you could tell he wanted to substitute me with literally anyone, even the school peon.

"Sorry, I can't run anymore. I'm feeling dizzy. I quit," I said, wiping the sweat off my forehead with my sleeve. I was still huffing.

"You can leave if you want, but why did you pick the ball with your hands?" Nitin snapped, his voice sharp enough to cut through the heat.

"Oh… actually…" I mumbled, not knowing what to say.

That's when my inner voice jumped in, dripping with sarcasm: *"Haan haan, admit it, Gopal. You did it on purpose so that poor Nitin couldn't score his golden goal."*

"Foul… Foul… by Gopal" Ravi, opponent captain declared…. "Please pass ball to my team, will take the penalty shoot" I said while looking at Nitin with smile.

Nitin gave me angry look, kicked the ground and then ran towards the centre and got into the game again.

I jogged up to our Sports Sir, still half out of breath.

"Dubey sir…" I puffed, "…sir, I'm not feeling well. Can I go to the classroom and rest a bit, please?"

"All okay?" he asked, raising his eyebrows.

Dubey sir glanced at his wrist. As always, it was hard to miss the golden *Rado* watch gleaming there. Everyone knew his obsession with watches, he had more models than our classroom had maps. Somehow, he always managed to 'arrange' those fancy brands that most Indians had only seen in magazines back then.

He barely waited for my reply. "Still fifteen minutes left for lunch break. Okay, you may go," he said, eyes already back on the football match.

I quietly walked back to the classroom to take some rest.

The classroom was supposed to be empty. But as I pushed open the door, I moved few steps inside and stopped. I saw Sandy and Sam sitting like kings at a feast, with not one, but five or six tiffin boxes spread out before them.

For a moment, I thought those were their own lunch boxes. But soon I realised they actually belonged to other students. They were happily sampling different cuisines, poha from one box, puri-sabzi from another, and someone's paneer paratha already disappearing into Sandy's bottomless stomach.

"GEM, you're here in the middle of the game? All okay?" Sam asked, his words coming out half-broken because his mouth was stuffed with a mix of every cuisine from the looted lunch boxes.

He chuckled, wiped his mouth with the back of his hand, and both of them happily went back to sampling food from one tiffin after another.

"Hey GEM, come on, today is International Buffet Day," Sam offered, waving a half-eaten puri like a trophy.

I shook my head. "No thanks." Honestly, my dizziness had killed my appetite, and besides, something about this scene screamed *trouble.*

So, I quietly walked to my desk, dropped my hands on the table, rested my forehead on them, and tried to sneak in a quick nap.

While I was trying to take a nap, I could hear their conversation as they kept eating, laughing, and giving reviews like restaurant critics "Gujarati food always has extra sugar in it… this Marwadi pickle is next level!" Once the boxes were completely wiped clean, they carefully placed each one back into its original bag, as if nothing had happened.

Just as they were about to leave, Sandy suddenly stopped at the door. He turned back, his voice firm. "GEM… listen."

Half-asleep, I lifted my head just enough to meet his eyes.

"We were not here when you came. Samjha? Hope you understood," he said in his usual blunt tone.

I gave a lazy nod and slipped back into my nap. The sleep weighing on me was stronger than any threat.

As they closed the door and moved towards the playground, I could hear Sam's fading anxious whisper, "What if someone goes and complains to Sharma sir?"

"Arrey, relax," Sandy replied with a sarcastic chuckle. "Sharma sir will handle it. After all, he's our tuition teacher."

The sound of their laughter thinned out, fading into silence as they left the building

The lunch bell rang, and the classroom filled with the usual noise of returning students. From my half-sleep, their chatter and footsteps felt like background noise in a dream.

Within minutes, noise turned into chaos.

From my desk, I heard rising cries—'My tiffin is empty!'… 'Even mine as well!' The same lines echoed around the classroom again and again.

"Gopal… Gopal!" Nitin shook me gently, trying to bring me back to my senses.

I slowly lifted my head, rubbed my eyes and tried to make sense of the chaos around me.

"You're burning, Gopal," Nitin said, pressing his hand on my forehead and then my arm, as if confirming I had a fever.

"Gopal… do you know anything about the incident? Who ate from those tiffins?" Nitin asked gently, mindful that I had fever.

"Ahhh… which incident?" I muttered in a broken, sleepy voice.

"Oh… okay, nothing Gopal. You just rest. I'll arrange some medicine for you," Nitin said gently before getting up and rejoining the group of students. My mind refused to make sense of the chaos, so I let sleep pull me back in.

I could faintly hear him telling the others near the door, "He's burning with fever and not even in his senses. There's no way he could have eaten seven or eight tiffins in this state. I don't think he's the one who did it."

After lunch, it was Yadav Sir's Geography period.

By then, everyone was back in the classroom, including the heroes of the chaos, Sandy and Sam. The room was pin-drop silent, though under the surface you could feel the tension. I had recovered a bit from the dizziness after taking some medicine during the break, but the atmosphere was still heavier than the summer heat outside.

Students were murmuring in low whispers, so faint that even the person on the next bench could barely catch a word. I glanced at Sandy. He casually winked at me with a smile, as if nothing had happened. His confidence reminded me of what he had told Sam earlier—that Sharma Sir would "take care of it."

Yadav Sir entered, and the class immediately stood up.

Before he could even begin, Nitin walked up to him and whispered for two or three minutes. Both of them glanced around at the students a couple of times during the conversation, which only added to the suspense.

When they were done, Yadav Sir gave a firm nod. Nitin went back to his seat.

"Sit down, class," Yadav Sir said. Then, without opening his book or touching the chalk, he walked straight to the door, looked outside, and stood there as though waiting for someone to arrive.

And then came the twist in the tale.

Through the door walked none other than our Principal, Mrs. Chitra Banerjee along with Sharma sir.

The moment she entered, the entire class froze. Mrs. Banerjee was famous across the school for her no-nonsense discipline. She had zero tolerance for mischief. Once, she had even suspended a student for a week, despite the fact that his parents were among the most influential in the city. That story alone was enough to keep every student on edge whenever she appeared.

How the hell did she come to know about this… and why is she here for such a small incident?" I faintly heard Sandy whisper to Sam.

Then, a moment later, his voice came again, this time loud enough to reach me. "Hey, Gopal…"

I looked up at him. Sandy's eyes locked on mine, and he gave a slight shake of his head. No words were needed, the gesture was enough to remind me of the threat he had already made earlier.

I ignored his look and turned my eyes back towards the Principal.

But Sandy bent forward and whispered in my ear, "Bhai… sun na."

That word—*Bhai*—took me by surprise. Just a while ago, this guy had been threatening me with glares, and now suddenly he was calling me *Bhai*. I didn't even know how to react.

He continued, his voice low and desperate. "Bhai… please, don't take our names. Last time she warned me in front of my parents, and now if she catches me again, she won't just suspend me… she'll throw me out. Please, brother… I promise, I'll give a treat to all the students whose tiffins we finished. Pukka promise."

The way he said it, I swear, if the classroom had been empty, he might have even touched my feet. For the first time, I could sense real anxiety on his face, his voice shaking with fear.

She was already suspecting who the culprits might be. Her sharp eyes scanned the classroom like a detective searching for clues. Then, in a stern voice, she demanded, "Who ate the lunch boxes? Tell me now."

The class fell into silence.

She walked slowly down the aisle and stopped right next to Sandy's bench. Fixing her gaze on him, she raised her voice, "I will not tolerate this kind of mischief in my school. Students should remember this clearly in their heads… understood, everyone?"

The whole class echoed nervously, "Yes, Madam."

I could see Sandy caught in a dilemma—not sure whether to look straight at Mrs. Banerjee or keep his eyes glued to the floor.

Then her voice boomed again, "Who is Gopal?"

"Present, Madam," I blurted out automatically, like it was roll call.

Inside my head, my inner voice screamed, *"Arrey duffer! Did you just say 'present, Madam' right now?"*

A faint ripple of laughter spread through the class.

"Sorry, Madam… I am Gopal," I corrected myself, raising my hand sheepishly.

"Gopal…" she stretched my name, as if trying to recall something. "Oh yes, you recently moved to Ahmedabad," she said.

"I heard you came back early from Sports because you were not feeling well?" she continued.

"Yes, Madam," I replied quickly. I didn't dare explain further—why invite more questions?

"You have a fever," she said, placing her hand lightly on my forehead.

"Yes, Madam. Nitin arranged some medicine. I'm feeling better now," I answered in the politest voice I could manage.

Her eyes narrowed. "So, your fever is gone now?" she asked, studying my face. That look made my heart skip—*was she suspecting me?* My thoughts tangled into knots.

Then came the blow. "Show me your lunch box."

Why does she want to see my lunch box… what will she find there? My head spun with confusion as I slowly pulled it out of my bag and opened it.

"You didn't eat your lunch, haan?" she asked again.

"Madam, I wasn't feeling well… I slept through lunch," I replied softly.

Her eyes stayed fixed on me. Then came the next question, sharper than before: "Did you see anyone inside the classroom when you came in?"

I took a deep breath and said, "Madam, when I came, the classroom was empty. I just sat down to rest. Maybe whoever did it came before me. I didn't see anyone." I forced my face to stay calm, though inside my heart was hammering.

She studied me closely for a few seconds, then exhaled and muttered under her breath about "notorious last benchers."

Before leaving, she raised her voice once more. "We will find out who the culprit is, and they will be punished." Her words hung in the air like a warning bell.

She turned towards the exit, Sharma Sir trailing behind her. As he walked out, he gave the class a sharp glare, pausing for the briefest moment at Sandy, just long enough to make the message clear.

The storm passed.

The whole day passed, but the air in the classroom never felt normal again. Teachers came and went, lessons were taught, but beneath it all, the tension of the lunch-box mystery kept floating around. Principal Madam even arranged lunch for the students whose tiffins had been looted by the LLB gang, yet the whispers and suspicion didn't stop.

"How are you feeling now?" Gayatri asked, handing me a tender coconut she had bought from the vendor near the bus stop.

I looked at her, a little surprised. She actually got coconut water for me?

By now, I think she must have guessed that my family's financial condition wasn't all that strong. I hardly ever had pocket money to spend in school, and gestures like buying coconut water were things I couldn't easily afford.

"Take it… you'll feel better," she said, pushing it gently but firmly into my hands.

"Oh, thanks… I'm fine now. I think it was just a sunstroke," I replied, sipping through the straw.

"Gopal..." I heard a voice from little far away.

It was Sam and Piddu coming running towards me. Sandy as usual was struggling even to walk fast.

They came close to us and stood there. Puffing and waiting for Sandy to arrive.

Finally, Sandy also came after a couple of minutes.

Sandy put both his hands on my shoulders.

"Bhai... Bhai" he said and hugged me.

I felt as if a ton of stinking flesh had been dumped on me.

"Thank you, bhai… thank you so much. You saved my career. Me and my coming generations will remain grateful to you for today…" Sandy said in a soft voice, a tone so unusual that for a second I wondered if it was really him.

"What???" Gayatri shouted in shock.

Sandy jumped, panicked, and quickly pressed his palm over her mouth while glancing around nervously. "Thand rakh, Mari Maan," he whispered anxiously.

Gayatri shoved his hand away. "Gopal… you knew it? And… you didn't…" she started, but before she could finish, I slowly nodded.

Then I took a deep breath and spoke, "Let me make one thing clear, Sandy. I lied not because you threatened me. I lied because if Principal Madam had caught you this time, she would have taken a stronger step—maybe even something that would have been disastrous for you and your parents. And yes… don't forget, you promised to give a treat to all those students whose tiffins you emptied. Remember that."

I exhaled, my words carrying both the weight of truth and the relief of finally saying it out loud.

"Yes, yes… gentleman's promise," Sandy said, nodding with a grin.

"Chalo, I'll give you both a samosa treat," he declared, grabbing both Gayatri's and my hands and pulling us towards the famous *Krishna Samosa Centre*.

"But… Gopal…" Gayatri tried to protest.

"Thand rakh, kudiye," Sandy interrupted, tugging harder this time, determined to drag us along.

That day, sitting with Sandy and the others at Krishna Samosa Centre, something shifted. I was no longer the outsider who had just joined school weeks ago. Whether I wanted it or not, I had found my place among the notorious Lords of the Last Benches.

The Great India-Pakistan Match Chaos

Present Day- 2025

A loud cheer sudden burst from the hall.

A chorus of laughter, clapping, and someone shouting, "Once more! Once more!"

The sound jolted me out of my thoughts.

I blinked, turned my head for a moment, and smiled faintly.

"Looks like Sara's gang has found a new target," I murmured.

The laughter faded, but that small interruption pulled me back to the present, to the half-open box sitting on the bed.

My eyes fell on something shiny among the papers, 'A silver disc- a movie CD'.

I let my hand rest on the silver shining CD for a second before picking it up.

It felt strangely cold, as if it had been waiting all these years just for me to pick it up. The light from the lamp bounced off its surface, and tiny rings of colour danced across the bedspread.

Amid that gentle shine, my old blue handwriting looked back at me, uneven and slightly smudged, yet full of confidence.

'18+'

I turned the disc over in my palm. It still had the same shine, refusing to age even though everything else had changed. For a moment, I saw my reflection in it, an older face, tired eyes, but the same smile from those days.

I blinked, and suddenly the room felt heavier. The laughter and music from the hall sounded fainter, distant, as if they belonged to another world.

I ran my thumb over the words again.

The ink had faded into a lighter shade, but the memory behind it hadn't.

It wasn't just a CD. It was a ticket back.

And somewhere deep inside, the reels began to turn.

School days- 1996

It was a Thursday afternoon, and the air in school already smelled of cricket. Every boy was whispering about the Sharjah Tri-Nation Trophy, 1996. It was India–Sri Lanka match that day.

According to some self-declared experts, if Sachin got out early, the whole of India should start fasting. Others claimed their uncle's neighbour's cousin was a Doordarshan cameraman, so they knew exactly how the pitch looked.

In the middle of this madness, Ashutosh, Ashu for us, decided he would not depend on anyone's uncle.

He came to our desk and gave a big smile.

"Guysssss..!!!" Ashu stretched the word so long it felt like he was announcing a train arrival at the station. His hand dived into the bag, and out came a small black object, wrapped in his handkerchief.

"You smuggled a transistor into school!" I blurted out, my voice at such a high decibel that at least half the class turned their heads.

Ashu, with the coolness of a film hero, placed it on the desk. "How can we miss the decider match between India and Sri Lanka? Whoever wins goes to the finals with Pakistan," he said, as if sneaking a transistor into school was the most natural thing in the world.

"The plan is simple," he said calmly, twisting the knob. "Hide it in the desk during Economics period, lean an ear close, and enjoy live commentary while pretending to study."

A couple of boys gasped. One whispered, "Is he crazy, Its Bhatia Madam's !"

Another said, *"Arre, if he gets caught, he'll be dead."*

But Ashu didn't care. He twisted the knob gently, and the transistor gave a faint crackle. A man's voice broke through the static, "...Kumble bowls, Jayasuriya pushes it to cover..."

Our eyes lit up. It was like holding the world's biggest secret. 30-40 students, all pretending to copy notes, but with ears stretched towards one small desk.

I whispered, *"You're the real Tendulkar, man. You just hit a century in school."*

Ashu grinned, *"Just chill, the volume's low. Madam won't even find out."*

And that's when fate, who clearly loved comedy, decided to intervene…

It all seemed like a masterstroke… until Bhatia Madam entered the picture.

Tall, thin, with a sharp nose, and a tongue even sharper. She believed her mission in life was to make economics feel like punishment. Her idea of motivation was saying things like, *"Tum logon se toh ek cycle ka demand supply bhi samajh nahi aayega. bas betho raho baratiyo ki tarah"*

Bhatia madam started dictating the concept of "The law of diminishing marginal utility"

Ashu desk was just before our desk. Ashu sat quietly, pretending to copy notes. His left ear bent towards the desk, catching every word from the tiny speaker.

Everyone knew that he is hearing commentary on the. He was giving live update to everyone with the hand gesture.

For a while, everything was smooth. Then, fate pressed the wrong button.

Suddenly, the volume knob twisted, and the transistor blared out like a loudspeaker:

"...AND THAT'S A FOURRR BY JAYASURYA!"

The class froze. For two seconds, there was silence. Then someone at the back whispered, "Another four by Jayasurya." A couple of boys giggled.

Ashu panicked, twisting the knob again. Instead of going down, the volume shot higher.

"India under pressure, fielders looking nervous..."

And nervous in the classroom too. Because Bhatia Madam's eyes were already drilling holes through Ashu's skull.

"ASHUTOSH!" She roared, *"Is this a movie show going on in class? Where is this noise coming from?"*

Ashu stood up, his face pale. "M-Ma'am... that is... that is a radio......"

Radio?!" she snatched it from his hand. "Is this a classroom or Eden Gardens? Why can't studies ever enter your brains? Your brains are always short in supply, just like money!"

The whole class was dead silent, but our shoulders were shaking from holding back laughter.

"Ma'am... today it's an important match... I just switched it on for a second... God promise," Ashu mumbled, his face full of innocence.

"Score? You've come here to watch the score or to study economics? Because of boys like you, the country is getting ruined! If you're so crazy about cricket, then wear your shoes, go to the street, spin the ball and hit a six! Have you come to school to play a match or what?"

She hit the transistor on the desk so hard even it let out a final dying crackle.

Ashu kept staring at the floor while Bhatia Madam went on hurling word-bombs one after another.

The class gasped. We had heard her sharp tongue before, but this was next level.

"Will go you to the principal's office right now" she ordered, dragging Ashu out by his arm.

The rest of us sat in silence, but the moment they stepped out, whispers started flying.

"Bro, now he'll be playing his second innings in front of the Principal."

By lunch break, Ashu was already the hero of the day. Except he didn't look like one. He was standing outside the Principal's office, knees bent, hands up in the air. His arms were trembling, face sweating. Every teacher passing by gave their own commentary.

Hindi Sir stopped, shook his head. "Forget studies, keep playing the radio. This is the new India."

PT Sir laughed, "Son, if you ever used this energy in a relay race, our school would have been famous by now."

Inside the class, we couldn't stop talking about it. Forget Sachin, forget Jayasurya. The real battle was Ashu versus Bhatia Madam. In the middle of all this madness, one thing was clear, cricket had completely taken over our school.

By the end of that chaotic transistor episode, Ashu's arms were shaking, Bhatia Madam was still fuming, and half the school had already heard about it. But honestly, none of us cared. Because by evening, India had won the decider against Sri Lanka. And that meant only one thing, India versus Pakistan in the finals.

The next morning, the whole class was buzzing like a fish market.

Ashu, still rubbing his sore arms, groaned, "At least my punishment was worth it. India won."

Sandy laughed, "Haan, and tomorrow your photo will come in the paper. Caption: *Boy sacrifices both hands for nation's victory.*"

Piddu added, "Next time, bring two transistors. One for commentary, epic soundtrack of your punishment scene."

Laughter spread across the whole class.

That's when Piddu jumped in, banging his desk like a judge. "Okay gang, listen up. Saturday evening, we must watch the final together."

Sandy shook his head. "Not at my place. My father treats this match like war. One sound, even cough, and he switches off the TV."

Piddu shrugged. "Come to my house. But warning, our TV is black and white. Sachin and Wasim Akram will both look like cousins from a 70s movie."

Everyone groaned.

Then Gayatri turned towards me. "What about your house, Gopal?"

I hesitated. "Actually, my parents are going to my uncle's place for a pooja. They'll stay overnight..."

Before I could finish, everyone cheered. "Perfect! Gopal's place it is!"

And right on cue came the favourite topic contribution.

Sandy rubbed his hands. "Okay. boys, ₹50 each. We need samosas, cold drinks, chips, and something heavy for dinner."

Before I could agree, Gayatri cut in, "Excuse me? He's already hosting. Why should he pay?"

The gang fell silent.

Piddu smirked, "Arre, look, Gopal's personal lawyer has taken over the case"

Gayatri didn't even blink. "Think about it. If the TV breaks, if uncle finds out, or the neighbours complain, whose head will roll? Gopal's. That's enough contribution."

I kept a straight face, but inside I was thanking every god on speed dial.

Sandy groaned, "Fine. Gopal is exempted. Rest of you pay ₹ 50, we'll manage the budget."

"Guys, just one thing, we need to remember my Nana isn't well. He'll be in his room," I said.

Everyone nodded, Sandy gave a big nod and smiled, the kind of smile that hides more than it shows.

"Guys… we'll all wear India jerseys for the match," Gayatri stood up and announced proudly.

Then she leaned closer to me and whispered, "I have an extra T-shirt of my brother. I'll bring it for you, no need to buy."

The plan was sealed. Saturday, 7 p.m., my house. India–Pakistan final. The biggest match of our lives.

While the rest of us went back to our normal routines, the LLB gang minus me had already shifted focus to their next secret project.

Sandy leaned over to Piddu during lunch. "Listen, cricket is fine, but finals ke pehle warm-up bhi zaroori hai."

Piddu raised his eyebrows. "Warm-up? You mean snacks?"

Sandy smirked. "Snacks toh Gayatri handle kar legi. I'm talking about something bigger. I have a few CDs hidden in our storeroom. The adult kind."

Sam almost choked on his aloo paratha. "You mean… those movies?"

"A perfect plot!" he declared, planting one leg dramatically on the bench. He waved his hands in the air like a film director setting up a shot. *"Scene one—LLB gang enters. Scene two—CD player on. Scene three—history created."*

Piddu clapped slowly. *"Wah, Spielberg of Shahibaug."*

Sam added, "Just remember, if we get caught, this will turn into a horror movie."

Piddu slapped the desk. "Genius! Gayatri and the girls will only come at 7 p.m. So, we'll meet at his place at 5. Cricket in the evening, and a warm-up match before that."

Sam hesitated, "But what about Gopal? He'll never agree."

Sandy winked. "That's why we won't tell him."

They all laughed, sealing the secret plan.

Saturday afternoon, i was taking a quick nap before everyone will come, I woke up to the sound of the doorbell. I checked the clock. 5 p.m. Who rings the bell now?

I dragged myself out of bed and opened the door, rubbing my eyes. And there they were, Sandy, Piddu, and Sam, all grinning like criminals caught red-handed.

"Surprise!" Sandy whispered loudly. "Warm up session before the match."

I blinked. "Warm up session......? You guys came too early?"

Immediately, I got the clue, whenever these three were huddled together, there had to be some secret conspiracy cooking.

"Guys, what are you up to?" I asked, almost sounding anxious.

Piddu pushed past me with a bag in hand. "Don't ask questions. Just let us in."

Sam followed, clutching a bundle of wires. "Trust me, this will be legendary."

I shut the door quickly, panic rising. "Guys, my Nana is sleeping inside. If he hears anything"

Sandy cut me off, patting my shoulder. "Relax. In our movie, we always keep it mute. No one will hear a thing."

I frowned. "Movie? What movie?"

Piddu gave a wicked smile, pulling out a shiny CD cover from his bag. I caught a glimpse of it and nearly fainted.

"You idiots!" I hissed. "You brought this here? What if someone finds out?"

Sam was already busy trying to set up the CD player with shaking hands. "Arre, don't worry. This is educational. Biology in motion."

"Education my foot!" I whispered angrily. "If Nana hears one scream, we're all finished."

Sandy grinned. "Don't worry, we're professionals. Mute button is our best friend."

They worked like a gang of smugglers setting up their contraband. The CD player hadn't been used in years, so it took fifteen minutes just to clean the dust. Wires were tangled, remote batteries dead, and the TV crackled like it was protesting.

"Arre, where's the AV button?" Sam whispered.

Piddu pressed random buttons until the screen flickered. Finally, the disc tray opened with a squeak. They shoved the CD in like it was a secret mission.

I stood near the door, sweating bullets. "I swear, if my Nana hears even one sound"

Sandy waved dismissively. "Mute mode on. Don't be so dramatic."

It took them 45–50 minutes, three arguments, two wrong wires, and one near electric shock to finally get everything working.

And with that, the forbidden movie began. On mute, of course. The three of them sat glued to the screen, eyes wide like they were watching the World Cup final already, while I kept pacing near the dining table half watchman, half detective, tracking any sign of Nana's movement from his room.

Inside, my stomach was already in knots, but not because of the movie.

Last night, Gayatri had called to plan for the big evening. She had her usual checklist voice, who's bringing snacks, what time to come, dinner plans. I was just nodding along, half-listening, when she suddenly dropped the real bomb.

"Oh, by the way, Nidhi will also join today."

I sat up straight. "Nidhi...? "

"She heard we're meeting at your place and practically begged me to bring her along," Gayatri explained. Then, after a pause, she added softly, "Honestly, I think she has a crush on you."

My jaw had almost hit the floor. "What? No way!"

"I'm serious" Gayatri said.

"You know very well, Gayatri. I'm not into all this, and honestly, I can't afford it either," I replied.

"I know, I know… you are such a *'Sidha Banda'*.... just be normal with her, okay?" she said.

And that was it. Gayatri being Gayatri, straightforward, no teasing, no drama. Only a true friend could drop such a bombshell in the middle of a conversation about the party.

So, while the LLB gang sat glued to their "warm-up match," my head kept echoing

Gayatri's words from last night, "*Sidha Banda*." And here I was, hosting three idiots watching an adult CD in my living room.

At around 6:15, the doorbell rang.

I whispered, "Must be the milkman or dhobi."

"Don't worry, the girls will take their time," Piddu declared, his eyes practically piercing into the screen.

I walked over lazily, and pulled it open without a care.

And froze.

"AHHHHHH!" I screamed, instantly slapping my right hand over my mouth like I'd just swallowed a firecracker.

Because right there, standing in front of me, were Gayatri and Nidhi.

Both staring at me with raised eyebrows.

The girls jumped at my scream. "What happened? Why are you shouting?"

Inside, chaos erupted. Sandy panicked, diving behind the sofa. "Remote! Remote! Where's the remote?"

"The remote is with me!" I yelled back, still blocking the doorway with both arms like a goalkeeper.

"Throw it!" Sandy shouted.

I panicked and lobbed the remote blindly behind me. Sandy leapt, but as usual with his heavy body, he missed. The remote hit the floor with a loud *thud*.

And that was the start of our comedy nightmare.

The remote, probably angry about being ignored for years, decided to malfunction. Sandy picked it up, pressed the "off" button… but instead of off, the mute button went off.

The TV suddenly unmuted. At first, the volume was still low, just a faint whisper of disaster.

Sandy jumped forward, hammering the remote. "Don't panic, I'll switch it off!"

"You moron, switch off the *player*!" Piddu snapped, eyes bulging.

"I'm trying!" Sandy hissed, sweat dripping.

But the CD player, clearly enjoying our misery, refused to obey. Sandy pressed the power button harder, as if brute force would help.

And that's when the nightmare doubled.

Instead of shutting down, the volume shot straight to full like the CD player also wanted its own climax.

The girl on screen let out a scream so loud it shook the window glass.

"Come on baby… YES… YES… I'm coming…!"

Now it wasn't just loud, it was deafening. The kind of sound that didn't just reach the neighbours, it probably alerted the entire postal code.

I swear, even the watchman down at the gate must have looked up, wondering which apartment had turned into a film set.

The three of them went into full panic mode, Piddu running in circles, Sam yanking cables, Sandy still stabbing the remote like it was a video game.

And me? I stood at the door, frozen, praying the earth would swallow me before Nana stepped out of his room.

"Switch it off!" Piddu cried,

"It's not working!" Sandy shouted back, pressing every button like he was defusing a bomb.

Piddu was running in circles, "Unplug it! Unplug it!"

Meanwhile, I stood at the door, arms stretched, desperately blocking the girls. "No entry! You… you can't come in right now!"

Gayatri's eyes narrowed. "What are you hiding, Gopal?"

Nidhi looked confused. "Why does it sound like… like……."

"NO! Don't say it!" I shouted, sweating like I'd run ten laps.

The woman on TV continued, her voice echoing across the colony. *"Yes… yes… faster… I'm coming!"*

It went on for two full minutes. The longest two minutes of my life.

Finally, in total desperation, I looked up at the power switch near the main door. Without thinking, I smacked it down.

Click.

Darkness. Silence. End of the nightmare.

Or so I thought.

From inside his room, my Nana's voice boomed, "What happened? Why are the lights off? And what was that....woman screaming?"

My heart nearly stopped.

Sandy whispered, "Tell him it was a movie trailer."

Sam hissed, "Tell him it was the neighbour fighting!"

I blurted out the first thing that came to mind. "Nana... woh... TV's volume button broke. Some random channel started playing... uhh... advertisement."

"Advertisement?!" Nana barked. "What kind of advertisement has a woman screaming like that?"

No one had an answer. We stood frozen.

After a long silence, Nana sighed. "Today's youth... I don't understand anything. Just switch on the light again. And keep it quiet!"

"Yes Nana!" we chorused like schoolboys caught stealing chalk.

Sandy quickly unplugged the CD player.

I flipped the switch back on. Lights came. TV stayed mercifully dead.

The girls finally walked in, both already giggling. Gayatri smirked, "So... this is how you boys do warm-up before a match?"

Nidhi tried to control her laughter but failed. "That poor woman...."

The whole gang burst out laughing, slapping each other, tears rolling down. The "incident" became bigger than the match itself.

By the time the India–Pakistan match finally began, our hearts were still racing from the "other" disaster of the evening. To be honest, the real drama had already happened in my living room. But still, when the first ball was bowled, the room went silent.

"Arre, this is it. History in the making," Sandy whispered, munching chips like it was prasad.

For the next few hours, the whole gang shouted, clapped, prayed, and abused the TV with full emotion. Every boundary by Sachin was treated like Diwali. Every wicket of Pakistan brought us to our feet. Even Nana, from his room, occasionally asked, "Kya hua? Kaun jeet raha hai?" and we'd shout back in chorus, "India!"

When the final run was hit and India sealed the victory, the house exploded. Chips flew, colas spilled, and voices cracked from screaming.

"INDIAAAA!!!" Piddu yelled, jumping on the sofa.

Piddu hugged Sandy so tight he nearly suffocated. "Bhai, we did it! We actually did it!"

Even Gayatri and Nidhi joined in, clapping and laughing.

We spilled out onto the streets where the entire colony had gathered. Firecrackers lit up the sky. Strangers hugged strangers. People danced like it was the biggest wedding ever.

Sandy, with his usual drama, raised his hands and shouted, "Boys, remember this night! The day we defeated Pakistan… and survived Gopal's house!"

We laughed till our stomachs hurt. We danced, screamed, and even cried a little. It wasn't only cricket we were celebrating it was the bond we had built. That night I realised something, no matter where life takes me, I might never get friends like this again. We were young, foolish, fearless, and together, and that was all that mattered. That night belonged to us. Friendship had won, and it felt like the greatest victory of all.

By the time we dragged ourselves back home, voices hoarse and legs aching, one thing was clear—this match would stay with us forever.

And just like that, three months of Class XII had flown by. From nervous new beginnings to transistor disasters to India's victory, everything felt like one long rollercoaster.

But school has its own way of reminding you that fun doesn't last forever.

The real match was waiting for us.

Surprise test

Present Day- 2025

I sat quietly on the bed, the open wooden box beside me.

I remained there, the open box beside me, my mind drifting, lost somewhere between then and now.

My eyes rested on the old CD, a small piece of a life that once seemed never-ending.

Just then, the door burst open.

A small boy ran in, out of breath, eyes wide. He slammed the door shut behind him and pressed his back against it.

"Shhh!" he whispered, giggling.

Before I could react, I heard voices outside, other kids shouting, "He's inside! Don't let him escape!" followed by loud footsteps running past the room. Three more kids came running in right after him, shouting, "Caught you! Caught you!"

They all tumbled into the room, laughing and jumping around.

"Sorry, Uncle!" one of them shouted as they all ran out again, still yelling, "Caught you! Caught you!" down the corridor.

And just like that, the room was quiet again.

The laughter faded, leaving behind only the faint echo of joy.

I sighed, smiling to myself.

My eyes went back to the box.

That's when I noticed it, a small, folded piece of paper lying near the corner.

The edges were soft, worn from years of being opened and closed.

I picked it up carefully, unfolded it slowly.

The paper felt fragile, like a piece of time that could crumble if I wasn't gentle.

Inside, in faded blue ink, were the words:

"Don't worry, keep smiling."

For a second, I just looked at it.

Then the corners of my mouth lifted, the same helpless smile from that day long ago.

Gayatri's handwriting, no doubt about it. Slightly tilted, a little uneven, but full of life.

I could almost see her again, standing by my desk, tearing a page from my notebook, scribbling these words, and sliding it toward me.

The sound of the kids' laughter still echoed faintly outside, but I barely heard it.

My world had already started to fade, the walls, the light, the present.

And before I knew it, I was back there again.

School days- 1996

The day after the India–Pakistan match felt like a hangover. Not from alcohol, but from cricket. Half the class was still replaying every six Sachin had hit, while the other half was crying about how their predictions failed. The transistor that Ashu had smuggled into school had turned into a class celebrity. Everyone wanted to touch it, like it was a lucky charm.

But the real storm was yet to come.

First period, our Economics teacher, Mrs. Bhatia, walked in. She never smiled, and today her face looked even more serious.

"Writing books out, not the textbook," she said, dumping her bag on the desk.

Everyone sat up straight. This tone was different. This wasn't the "let's open Chapter 4" tone. This was the "time to ruin your day" tone.

She picked up the chalk, wrote in big capital letters: SURPRISE TEST.

The class gasped. Some even said "Arre baap re" loud enough to echo. Sandy looked at Sam as if he'd just been told to run 10 km with PT Sir.

"Today, 50 marks test. No excuses, sit quietly." Her voice had the sweetness of karela juice.

Sandy and Sam, the official last bench brand ambassadors, were her first target.

"You two, come in front. First bench."

Their faces dropped. Sitting on the first bench was like being punished to watch a cricket match on Doordarshan while your friends cheered in the stadium.

"Ma'am . . . but—" Sam tried to protest.

"No but. No excuse. Sit."

Both dragged themselves forward, looking like prisoners shifting jails. The class giggled, enjoying the rare sight of the kings of the back bench now under full CCTV surveillance.

Meanwhile, Piddu, the master of disguise, managed to stay invisible. He quietly adjusted himself behind a taller boy and escaped her radar. Pure survival instinct.

She distributed the question papers with a dramatic pause, as if each paper carried not questions but arrest warrants.

But Sandy and Sam? Their faces screamed "SOS." Sandy stared at the paper like it was written in Sanskrit, and Sam started chewing his pen cap as if it might leak answers.

The teacher walked around with her hawk eyes.

"No whispering. No looking around. And yes, I am watching."

One boy muttered under his breath, “Even ISRO doesn’t track satellites this closely.” The class snorted but quickly went silent when she glared.

Every tick of the clock felt louder.

That’s how the day began. A cricket hangover, a surprise Economics test, and Sandy and Sam sitting on the first bench like punished kids.

She clapped to mark the start of the period, but in our class the only sound was the scratching of pens. For once, even the notorious last benchers were forced into silence.

I tried to keep my focus on the paper. The first two questions were not too bad. Somehow, I managed to remember a few lines from last week’s reading. Words started flowing, not like poetry, but at least enough to fill a page.

Gayatri, as usual, was in top gear. Her head was bent low, hand moving so fast it looked like she was racing the clock. She had this neat habit of writing in perfect margins, as if her answers were meant for a textbook.

Some others in the class were also doing fine. A few had their tongues sticking out, like it helped them remember better. One boy tapped his pen against his forehead after every line, as if he was trying to knock answers out of his brain.

But the real comedy was right in front.

Sandy had written his name in bold and then stopped, staring at the question paper as if it had betrayed him. He tilted his head left, then right, like the words might make sense from another angle.

Sam, on the other hand, was no better. He chewed the pen cap till it looked like a dog toy. He wrote something, scratched it out, then wrote again. His page looked more like a railway timetable filled with cancellations.

At one point, Sandy leaned towards Sam, whispering, “Sam, what’s question two?”

Before Sam could react, the teacher’s voice cut through the air.

"Quiet! No talking."

Sandy froze, pretending to adjust his collar, while Sam dropped his pen on the floor and bent down, trying to look innocent. The class chuckled quietly.

Meanwhile, Piddu at the back was enjoying himself. He had slipped under the teacher's radar completely. From his seat, he managed to tilt his head just enough to peep into my answer sheet on the left and Nitin's on the right. His eyes moved quicker than his pen. Whatever he saw, he copied without shame, mixing the two answers together like a chef creating a fusion dish.

Every now and then, he looked up, smiled, and went back to writing as if everything was his own idea. Nobody noticed, except a few of us, who shook our heads and laughed silently. That boy had a talent for survival. Sometimes he even gave us a small thumb-up, like a commentator encouraging a losing team.

The tension in the room was funny. Everyone was fighting their own battle. Some pressed their pens so hard that the nib tore the paper. Others kept flipping the sheet, hoping that the back page had easier questions.

The teacher's heels clicked on the floor as she moved up and down the aisles. Each step sounded louder than the last. Every time she stopped, shoulders stiffened, eyes dropped, and even the loudest boys turned into saints.

Sandy tried a new trick. He drew arrows from one answer to another, connecting random lines, as if flowcharts would impress her. Sam started filling the page with long sentences that made no sense but looked serious. If you read them, you would find words like "economics," "growth," "important," and "very necessary" sprinkled everywhere.

The clock ticked slowly, adding pressure with every minute. Sweat patches appeared on uniforms. A few heads went down on the desk, resting for two seconds before starting again.

Finally, the teacher's voice broke the silence.

"Last five minutes. Finish your answers."

The class went into overdrive. Pens scratched faster, papers flipped, and the sound of rapid writing filled the room. It was like a last-minute exam race where everyone suddenly found energy.

Sandy looked at his paper, sighed, and then quickly filled the last half page with giant handwriting. Sam followed the same trick. The bigger the letters, the fewer the lines.

And then came the final order.

"Stop writing. Pass your sheets forward."

A wave of relief spread across the room. Some leaned back, some stretched their arms, others closed their eyes like they had finished a marathon.

But not Sandy and Sam. Their faces told a different story. They looked like two boys who had gone to war with wooden swords.

"Stop writing. Pass your papers forward," the teacher said, in a voice that left no room for mercy.

Sheets started moving up row by row. Some boys looked proud, some looked scared, and a few looked as if they were handing over their will to the police.

Sandy stretched his arm, gave one last glance at his half-filled paper, and muttered, "Goodbye, my dear." Sam sighed loudly, as if his soul had left with the paper.

The teacher gathered all the sheets into one neat stack. She tapped them twice on the desk, dusted her hands, and looked at the class.

"Most of you tried. I will check and tell," she said, her eyes scanning. Then her voice hardened. "But some of you… you didn't even attempt properly."

Everyone froze. We knew exactly where this was heading.

Her eyes went straight to the first bench.

"You two," she pointed at Sandy and Sam, "what were you writing? Was it Economics or comedy script?"

The class burst out laughing but quickly stopped when she raised her hand.

Sandy tried his innocent face. "Ma'am, I... I studied but..."

"But what?" she snapped. "Your paper looked like a shopping list. And you," she turned to Sam, "half your answers are the same sentence repeated three times."

Sam scratched his head. "Ma'am... I was just... emphasising the point."

Her voice rose. "Emphasising? This is not drama class! This is Economics!"

The classroom shook with her anger. Even the ceiling fans seemed to slow down.

"You both are always at the back, laughing, disturbing others. Today you sat in the front, and still this is what you do?" She slammed the papers on the desk.

Sandy and Sam lowered their heads, staring at the floor.

"You should be ashamed," she continued, her words sharp. "Other students managed. Even those who didn't know much at least tried sincerely. But you two... are wasting time."

The silence after her words was heavy. No one moved, no one whispered.

From the back, Piddu had escaped her eyes once again.

Gayatri looked worried. She hated public scolding, even if it wasn't for her. Some others tried hard not to laugh at the situation. A few actually felt bad for Sandy and Sam, but no one dared to say anything.

"Next time," the teacher warned, "if you come unprepared, I will throw you out of class."

That final line hung in the air like a death sentence.

She picked up the stack of answer sheets, adjusted her sari, and walked out of the classroom with quick steps. The sound of her heels faded down the corridor.

The moment she left, the entire class burst into whispers.

"Madam was on full fire today."

Sandy leaned back, looked at Sam, and whispered, "We can't take this, yaar."

Sam nodded. "She insulted us too much."

Their faces were no longer embarrassed. They had changed into the familiar look of plotting mischief. The kind of look that usually ended with trouble for the entire school.

And that's how the seeds of revenge were planted, right in the middle of our Economics period.

The lunch bell rang, and the classroom suddenly came alive again. Steel tiffin boxes opened, smells of poha, paratha, and pickle mixed in the air.

But Sandy and Sam sat quietly, still sulking.

Sandy finally said, "She insulted us in front of everyone."

Sam nodded, poking his roti with a finger. "We can't let this go."

They looked at each other. The spark was clear. Trouble was loading.

From behind, Piddu leaned backward, munching on Gayatri's Aaloo paratha he had somehow grabbed. "What are you both cooking?"

Sandy whispered, "Revenge."

Sam added, "Big revenge."

Piddu chuckled. "Oh ho, madam vs. you two… this will be fun. But what's the plan?"

That's when Sandy's eyes lit up. He pointed towards the corridor wall. A tiny lizard was clinging upside down, its tail twitching.

"See that?" Sandy whispered dramatically, like a movie villain revealing his weapon.

Sam's jaw dropped. "Lizard?"

"Yes," Sandy grinned. "That's the plan."

Sam blinked. "You mean…?"

"Exactly. Madam's purse."

For a moment, Sam looked horrified. Then slowly, a wicked smile spread across his face. "Brilliant."

Now came the operation. Sandy took out his handkerchief, folded it twice like a hunter preparing a trap. He tiptoed to the wall. The lizard twitched again. A couple of classmates noticed and held their breath, enjoying the live show.

"Careful, careful," Sam whispered loudly, which of course attracted more attention.

Sandy lunged, clapped the handkerchief against the wall, and held it tight. The lizard wriggled inside. The class erupted in muffled laughter, covering their mouths with tiffin lids.

Sandy returned like a hero carrying treasure. He held the squirming bundle up for Sam. "Target locked."

Sam looked nervous but excited. "Now the staffroom, it's lunch time and everyone would be in the pantry… no one will be there."

During lunch hour, most teachers went to the pantry for tea and snacks. The staffroom was almost empty, except for a few bags and purses hanging from the chair handles.

The three of them sneaked down the corridor. Sandy led, Sam followed, and Piddu tagged along just for the entertainment.

They peeked inside. Empty. Perfect timing.

Madam's brown leather purse was lying open on the table, the zip half undone.

Sandy looked at Sam. "Ready?"

Sam nodded, holding the handkerchief as if it contained a bomb.

In one swift move, Sam pulled the zip wider, Sandy dropped the lizard inside, and Piddu quickly closed it.

Done. Mission successful.

They ran out, trying not to laugh. Once back near the staircase, they burst into silent giggles, their shoulders shaking.

Piddu whispered, "This is history. Tomorrow, they'll write about this in the school magazine."

Sandy smirked. "Forget the magazine. This will go down as a legend."

And so the trap was set. Madam had no idea her purse now carried more than chalk, pens, and handkerchiefs. It carried the perfect recipe for chaos.

The trap was set. Sandy, Sam, and Piddu spent the rest of the lunch break giggling like thieves who had just looted a bank. Every time the purse came to their mind, they looked at each other and burst into silent laughter.

The bell rang. Students rushed back to class. Some carried their tiffins half-eaten, some still chewing, and a few dragging their feet because the break was too short. But Sandy and Sam were unusually fresh. Their eyes sparkled with excitement.

Fifteen minutes later, our Bhatia madam returned. She walked in with her usual authority, adjusting her attire, and dropped her chalk box on the table. She looked calmer than in the morning, probably after some tea.

Then came the moment.

She reached into her purse to take out her red pen. Her hand slid inside, searching. For two seconds, nothing. Then her face changed. Her eyes widened, her mouth opened, and suddenly a scream tore through the classroom.

"AAAAAHHHHHHHHHH!"

The sound was so loud even the next class peeped in. She flung the purse on the desk, stumbling back as if it had exploded. The lizard jumped out, tail twitching, and ran straight across the desk.

Madam's hands went to her head. She swayed once, then fainted right there on the chair.

For a moment, silence. Then absolute chaos.

One boy shouted, "Get water!" Another ran to the corridor yelling, "Teacher fainted! Teacher fainted!" Within seconds, the news spread like wildfire across the school.

From the window, we saw students from other classes already gathering, trying to peek in. Some thought it was a fire drill, others thought someone had brought a snake.

Inside the class, our own boys were torn between helping Madam or panicking.

In the middle of all this, Sandy and Sam sat at the back, their faces red from holding in laughter. Sam pressed his stomach, whispering, "I can't… I'll burst." Sandy covered his mouth with both hands, shaking so hard his bench rattled.

Piddu leaned over, grinning. "Mission successful, boss."

Soon, two senior teachers rushed in with a bottle of water. One sprinkled a little on Madam's face, another fanned her with a notebook. Slowly, she opened her eyes, still shivering.

"What… what was that?" she whispered.

"Madam, lizard," someone replied.

Her face turned pale again. She refused to touch her purse, as if it was cursed forever.

The bell rang to mark the end of the period, but no one cared about the next class. All the corridors were buzzing with just one topic – *Bhatia Madam fainted because of a lizard in her purse.*

By evening, it had already become the school gossip of the year. Every version was more dramatic than the last. Some said it was a snake, others swore it was a giant lizard, and a few added masala, claiming she fainted twice.

But the truth was known to only three boys. And out of them, two laughed so much their stomachs hurt – Sandy and Sam, the proud inventors of the greatest prank of our school year.

But in school, happiness always comes with a warning. Just when you start to enjoy the victory, another storm is already building in the background.

And none of us knew that another storm waiting for us… was another surprise test.

Our first school bunk

That morning started like any other. Gayatri and I reached on time to the school.

While entering the school gate, I burped bit loudly "Oops… Sorry… my stomach is doing somersaults" i said while putting my hand to cover my mouth.

Now, usually whenever we spotted Chauhan Sir, the English teacher, anywhere, the rule was simple, change direction immediately. Cross the road, hide behind whatever you find, pretend to tie shoelaces, anything. No student in their right mind willingly crossed paths with him.

But as luck would have it, he was standing right near us. We had no choice but to greet him. 'Good morning, sir,' we both said… and that's exactly when I burped loudly. Sometimes fate doesn't just test your faith, it laughs at it as well."

Chauhan sir, with his tall frame, ironed trousers, and permanently angry eyebrows, simply nodded with changed facial expression because of my burp. But that single nod felt like a death sentence.

"Take care, son," he said, with full base in his voice. Then, before he could even react, I marched quickly towards the building entrance.

The terror of Chauhan sir was not some myth, it was daily reality. His stick, polished so well it looked like he applied mustard oil every night, had cracked more palms than the cricket bats on our school ground. He didn't shout much, he didn't even waste time threatening. But when his voice went silent, the whole class automatically started praying, because silence meant his "Danda" was about to do the talking. And by the name itself you can guess what it was used for. The most horrifying sentence in the life of any KVS student was when Chauhan sir would suddenly say, "Get my Danda."

By the time I reached class XII-C, the rumour had already travelled faster than the morning assembly prayer. Chauhan sir's own son, who studied in the science stream, had leaked the news: there would be a surprise English test today.

"ENGLISH SURPRISE TEST!" someone whispered loudly near the backbench.

"Today? A surprise one?" another boy asked, eyes wide.

"Yes, confirmed news from Chauhan's son," the reply came like breaking headlines.

The word "surprise" itself spread like an earthquake tremor, shaking weak students like me who were still traumatised from the economics test incident a few weeks ago.

In that economics test, the senior member of the LLB gang had performed so badly that Bhatia madam nearly got a blood pressure check done right there.

And that incident was enough to make them promise they would never again sit helpless in a surprise test.

So when the English test rumour came, Sandy's face tightened with worry. He leaned forward, whispering just loud enough for the LLB gang to hear, "This is it. We're not going to repeat economics, and that too in English.... NEVER..... He paused and dropped the bomb "Today, we will bunk the school."

The word "bunk" hit me like thunder. My ears turned hot, my palms sweaty. I had never bunked in my life. I was kind of a "good boy," the one who still raised his hand to ask permission for a glass of water.

I wanted to avoid this. My mind was running through a million excuses. Finally, I blurted out, "But I greeted Chauhan sir this morning! What if he remembers me?"

Sandy rolled his eyes so dramatically. "Arre idiot, everyday two hundred students greet him. You think he has CCTV inside his brain?"

Sam giggled, "Yes, he doesn't even remember his own period timetable half the time, forget your good morning."

Piddu added with his usual humour, "If he remembered every kid who greeted him, he would've been in CBI, not teaching English."

The three of them burst into muffled laughter, while I sat there imagining Chauhan sir's angry face in slow motion, holding his baton like a police inspector about to begin third-degree interrogation.

The classroom atmosphere was buzzing. Some were genuinely opening books, trying to glance through grammar rules in thirty minutes, as if suddenly they would master every tense from past, present, and future at once.

One boy shouted from the front, "Arre, anyone remember which question he asked last time?"

Sandy replied, "Yes! 'To bunk, or not to bunk, that is the question!'"

The whole row snickered. Even in fear, humour was our oxygen.

Piddu in his dramatic voice said, " Look outside the window, the mild morning sun, the peepal tree near the wall with had fresh green leaves, and the dust rising from a distant cricket match looked like a golden mist. It almost looks as though nature is whispering, "Don't sit here, children. Run, be free."

Sandy caught that look in my eyes. He leaned closer, whispering in a mock-dramatic tone, "See, even God is signalling. This is the day, my friend. Today you'll become a true LLB gang."

"What a fish," I muttered weakly.

Sam patted my back, "Don't worry. By evening, you'll thank us."

Piddu, stretching like he had already finished the test, declared, "Confirmed. Today is history in the making."

The bell for the morning assembly rang. Instead of calming us, it only added to the tension.

Whispers about the English test kept circling, and every knock on the door made us jolt as if a police inspector was about to raid the class.

I could see Sandy scribbling something on the last page of his notebook. He was drawing a crude map of the school with an arrow pointing towards what he called the "secret exit."

"This," Sandy tapped the paper, "is our way to freedom."

Sam's eyes sparkled, "Back lane escape?"

Sandy nodded.

Piddu clapped softly, "Wah, like a jailbreak. Just missing the background music."

I sat frozen, staring at the map, feeling like a kidnapped soldier forced to join the enemy.

But somewhere deep inside, a tiny spark of excitement flickered. The idea of walking out, free of tests, free of Chauhan sir's , questioning, free of English grammar, it pulled at me. It felt wrong, dangerous, but also thrilling.

And then I looked at Gayatri, sitting a few benches ahead, happily making notes with her colourful pens. That sight made me gulp. After this bunk, she'd mark me as officially corrupted by Sandy and Sam from 'Sidha Banda' itself. That thought scared me almost as much as Chauhan sir's glare.

"Guys.. I don't think I would be able to do it," I said with anxiety

"You don't have option now…" Sandy said while staring at the map.

Now the decision wasn't in my hands anymore. Sandy had already folded the map, slid it into his pocket, and grinned like a politician after passing a secret bill.

The plan was set. The rumour had done its job.

The day of my first bunk had officially begun.

Sandy whispered, "Okay, listen carefully. We'll use the secret exit. Near the cycle stand, behind the old banyan tree, there's a broken part of the wall. It's been there for years, but only a few know about it. We jump from there."

Sam's eyes widened. "But what if peon catches us?"

"Arre yaar," Sandy rolled his eyes, "in the morning he would be busy in managing the morning assembly stuff. Don't worry."

Piddu grinned, "And if he shows up, we'll tell him we're doing survey of cracks in the wall for Geography project."

Sandy added, "Don't worry we are cigarette buddies as well… he is harmless"

They laughed quietly. My throat went dry. I whispered, "Guys, this is risky. What if someone tells Chauhan sir?"

Sandy looked at me with his trademark don't-care expression. "Who will tell? Here all our brothers and...... your sisters too," he said, giving a mischievous wink.

I wasn't convinced. My heart was thudding like tabla in Ganesh Visarjan.

Sandy tapped his watch. "Okay, plan is simple. At the time of the assembly, when everyone is marching towards the playground, there will be a rush in corridors. We'll slip out, go straight to the cycle stand, jump the wall, and take the back lane. Easy."

"Easy for you," I muttered, "my father will kill me if he finds out."

Piddu leaned back casually, "Relax, GEM. Everyone bunks one day or the other. Your day has come. Don't act like you're going for war."

The three of them burst out laughing. I forced a smile, but inside I was already seeing my obituary printed in the newspaper: *'Student caught bunking. Father performs last rites with his chappal.'*

The bell rang. That moment, my life split in two halves, the obedient student who wanted to stay, and the trembling adventurer who was being dragged by Sandy's strong grip.

"Chal!" Sandy whispered, grabbing my arm.

Before I could protest, Sam and Piddu were already tiptoeing towards the door. The corridor was full of students rushing towards the ground. We merged into the crowd like four undercover agents. My legs felt like jelly, my palms cold. Every teacher who passed us looked like a jailor about to blow the whistle.

Finally, we reached the cycle stand. Sandy pointed to the old banyan tree. Behind it, there really was a broken patch of wall, half-hidden by creepers.

Piddu clapped softly, "Wah, secret gate of heaven!"

Sam looked around nervously. "Anyone watching?"

Sandy shook his head, "No one. Go."

Before I could blink, Sandy had already climbed halfway and jumped to the other side. Sam followed, tumbling like a sack of potatoes but landing safe. Piddu climbed with style, shouting, "freedom from the surprise test!" as he leaped.

Now it was my turn. My legs refused to move.

"Arre jaldi!" Sandy hissed from the other side.

"I can't!" I whispered back, sweating.

"Tell me the rules of the past participle tense" Sam teased.

That was enough. With heart pounding, I scrambled up the wall, tore my pants near the knee, and jumped. I landed flat, dust flying, but alive. The four of us stood there, outside the school boundary, breathing hard.

Piddu spread his arms dramatically, "Gentlemen, welcome to freedom!"

We all laughed nervously. For the first time, the school building behind us looked like a prison we had just escaped from.

The back lane stretched ahead, dusty and quiet, leading towards the main road. Rickshaws rattled past, a buffalo lazily chewed cud near a garbage heap, and the world outside felt strangely brighter.

The school bell was still ringing faintly behind us, echoing like a warning, but here, beyond the wall, we felt untouchable.

Piddu spread his arms wide like Shahrukh Khan in *Dilwale Dulhania Le Jayenge*. "Gentlemen," he announced, "welcome to independence. We are no longer students. We are free men."

Sandy laughed, "Shut up, idiot. You're still wearing uniform. Free man my foot….."

Sam chuckled nervously, "But really, it feels different, no? Like the air is lighter here."

I nodded slowly. He was right. Even the smell of the dust and diesel from passing rickshaws felt better than the chalk powder and the blackboard duster inside the classroom. My heartbeat, which had been racing like a horse till now, started to slow down. For the first time that day, I smiled without fear.

Sandy grinned, "Now the plan. Movie. *Hum Aapke Hain Koun.* Roopalee Cinema… we'll watch the 12 noon show so that we can reach home at our usual school time"

Sam's eyes lit up, "Yes! And samosas before interval!"

How come anything go so smooth when LLB gang is together.

And here Piddu goes again.

Piddu tilted his chin, acting cool. "But one condition. We will go only if we get lift in a premium car. Not any auto or scooter. Premium only."

"Premium car? We've just bunked school, we need to get out of sight quickly… and this moron wants a premium car, seriously!" I thought furiously.

"Forget about premium, if any normal car gives a lift it would be a miracle," Sandy said

But Piddu was stubborn. He folded his arms, "Only premium. Otherwise, not worth our first bunk."

Sandy slapped his forehead, "This idiot will make us walk ten kilometres in the sun."

I shook my head, laughing. "You'll see. Nobody will stop."

We stood there by the side of the main road, four boys in half-pants, sweating, sticking out our thumbs every time a car passed. Most drivers ignored us. One scooter slowed down, looked at us, and sped away as if we were thieves.

"See?" Sandy muttered. "Your premium condition will kill us."

But just then, as if God himself was in mood for comedy, a shining black Mercedes slowed and stopped right in front of us.

Our jaws dropped. The silver star on the bonnet glittered like it was laughing at us.

Piddu whispered dramatically, "Behold... destiny."

The window rolled down. A man in his late thirties, wearing sunglasses and a crisp white shirt, leaned out. "What are you boys doing here in uniform? Shouldn't you be in school?"

My mind started calculating the risk ... "Is he a teacher of our school.... No way he is in Mercedes my friend." My inner voice was also making fun of it.

For a second, no one spoke. Our throats were dry. Then Sandy coughed and mumbled, "Sir... we are going for group study. Nearby only."

The man raised an eyebrow. "Group study in a cinema hall?"

Sam gasped, "How do you know?" Then quickly covered his mouth.

The man laughed heartily. And said the most common dialogue most Indian have spoken in this kind of situation "I am the principal of the school in which you are students, you think I never bunked school? Same broken wall. Same fear of getting caught. You boys reminded me of my own days."

We all looked at each other, stunned. Was he serious?

He smiled, "Come, sit. I'll drop you near the cinema hall....Which Cinema hall and which movie?"

Sandy hesitated. "Really, sir?.. We are planning to watch 'Hum Aapke Hain Kaun' at Roopalee cinema"

"Come on in," the man nodded. "But one advice. Always carry an extra T-shirt in your bag. Change it before going out. Otherwise anyone will recognise you as schoolboys. At least then you'll look like college bunkers, not kids."

Piddu's eyes sparkled. "Sir, genius! Extra T-shirt, noted."

Sam whispered, "Wah, premium car *and* premium advice."

We climbed into the backseat, Sandy took the front seat. Our excitement bubbling. The leather seat felt smoother than our classroom benches. I pressed my palm against it and thought, *This is definitely worth a few slaps tomorrow.*

As the car glided down the road, Piddu leaned back dramatically. "This is life. Bunking school in Mercedes. Kya din hai."

Sandy snorted, "Stop acting like a Nawab. You'll still eat a 2-rupee samosa in the cinema canteen."

We laughed till our stomachs hurt.

The man chatted with us on the way, sharing stories of how he once bunked to watch *Tridev* and got caught by his uncle in the same theatre. "My ears are still ringing from the beating," he said, laughing. "But trust me, boys, these memories stay with you longer than marks in any test."

His words hit me. I leaned back, looking out at the city rushing by, and felt something shift inside me. This wasn't just about running away from

Chauhan sir's or the English test. It was about doing something silly with friends that we would remember for years.

When the car stopped near the cinema hall, we thanked him. He waved casually. "Enjoy, boys. And don't forget the T-shirt advice."

As the Mercedes pulled away, leaving a trail of dust, Piddu puffed out his chest. "See? I told you. Premium or nothing. History written."

Sandy laughed, "History, yes. But tomorrow Chauhan sir will write geography on your back with ."

Sam clapped his hands, "Forget tomorrow! Today we are kings. Come, Madhuri Dixit is waiting, Didi tera devar deewana........"

We marched towards the theatre, four boys with empty pockets but hearts bursting with joy.

For me, each step felt heavier with thrill. It was wrong, it was risky, it was stupid. But it was also unforgettable. My first bunk, my first moment of living outside rules.

And as we bought balcony tickets with our pooled money less contributed by me, I thought silently, *Maybe, just maybe, some mistakes are worth making.*

The next morning, I walked into class with the same sinking feeling. My body was present, but my soul had already booked a hospital bed. The entire night, I went through a mix of feelings, I kept replaying that moment on the road, Chauhan sir's piercing eyes, his silence, my burp.

The bell rang. Everyone stood up for the morning greeting. It was English period. My heart was sinking with every bad thought possible.

"What if Chauhan got to know about our bunk, what if he remembered my morning greeting...." All the what -ifs danced wildly in my head.

Usually, Murphy's Law, "if anything can go wrong, it will go wrong", seems to find me without much effort

Chauhan sir entered the class room with his usual walk. Everyone stood up for the morning greeting.

He nodded as if he were fulfilling an obligation.

He glanced around like a police inspector entering a gambling den. His eye got locked onto our bench.

Without a single word, he told to the class monitor, "Get my Danda."

The class froze.

And there it was, the dreaded stick, shining as if it had been polished specially for our funeral.

Sandy leaned towards me and muttered under his breath, "Lag gaye… interval khatam, second half starts."

Sam's lips quivered. "Should I faint now itself?"

Piddu whispered dramatically, "Remember boys, dignity in defeat."

Before I could even react, Chauhan sir walked to Sandy's desk. No questions, no accusations, no suspense. Just *THWACK*. One clean shot on each hand. Sandy winced, but didn't cry. He simply held his palms out.

Sam was next. *THWACK*. His hands turned red instantly. He bit his lip, looking like he might burst into tears any second, but he stayed quiet.

"Pradeep!" Chauhan sir's voice boomed. "Stand up."

Piddu, always the actor, stood as though he were stepping on stage. "Yes, sir?"

"Speak. Small essay. India–Pakistan match."

The class went pin-drop silent. Everyone turned to watch. And then, in his broken, hilarious English, Piddu began:

"Sir… yesterday match was very, very… tension. India batting first. Azharuddin looking like… hero, but out like… zero. Then Sachin, sir… Sachin play like God, but also God sometimes needs rest, so he also out. Pakistan bowling, sir, was fast like… scooter without brake. Finally India made runs, but not made enough runs. Then Pakistan batting… Inzamam looking like… big buffalo running… but also hitting fours. Whole India crying, sir. Neighbours also crying. Even my dog didn't eat food yesterday."

The class was dying inside, shoulders shaking to hold in laughter. But nobody dared to let a sound escape. Chauhan sir's face was stone, unreadable.

THWACK. One clean shot on each hand.

"Kuch padha hota toh aata na?" He said, his face red with anger.

Then he turned to me. My stomach flipped.

This time he changed his stance… he put the Danda down on the desk… and started folding his sleeves.

"You," he said. "Correct grammar mistakes here, 'He were there, They were there and we was there'"

I stood up, throat dry, palms sweating. My brain was blanker than a new notebook. I tried, "Sir… umm…"

"Quickly…. we don't have whole day to wait" He said while playing with Dandas. That made me more nervous… My brain is kind of going in the hibernation mode…..

'Yes sir…. Yes sir….. sir it should be 'He were being there'….."

Before I could proceed, *SLAP*. Right cheek.

The slap was so hard that i got completely blank for few seconds, i could hear the whistling sound in my both the hear. I tried to stand straight.

"Sorry sir…." I kept looking at the floor.

"Correct grammar… come on" He said with more anger.

"He… he… was there…. They…. were there…." I said.

Again, before I could proceed, *SLAP*. Right cheek.

Now I lost sense of what to say... I was randomly trying my luck with different sentences and every time before i finished, I got a tight SLAP on my right cheek, it was like a machine gun firing.

I remember I counted around sixteen SLAP….. yes sixteen tight SLAPS….. before the numbers blurred.

And then, something unexpected happened.

From the front row, Gayatri's voice rang out "Sir, it should be 'He was there, They were there and We were there"."

The class gasped.

She looked at me, I couldn't meet her eyes and continued looking at the ground.

"You were not supposed to speak Gayatri" he said at the top of his voice. It was no less than a lion roar.

He went to Gayatri "Who told you to speak".

Before she could answer, he swung the Danda on her palm. Once. Twice. Gayatri flinched but stood firm, her face defiant. I could see her eyes filled with tears, but she controlled them from failing.

My heart twisted. She didn't have to speak. She could have stayed quiet, let me drown alone. But she hadn't. She had stepped in, and now she too was paying the price.

Chauhan sir turned back to me. His voice boomed so the whole class could hear. "You burped while greeting me yesterday morning. Correct Gopal?, you four bunked my class"

The LLB gang froze. Even Sandy, who usually grinned in the face of punishment, looked pale. The entire class turned to stare at me. My ears, still burning from the slaps, turned hotter. My shame was complete.

"I want 100% attendance in my class… hope that's understood loud and clear by everyone," he announced glancing everyone in the class.

The bell rang. Period over. Chauhan sir dropped the Danda on the desk with a loud *thunk* and walked out without looking back.

The silence that followed was deafening. Then whispers erupted, like a gossip monsoon flooding the room.

"More than sixteen slaps!" someone muttered.

"Gayatri also got hit," another whispered.

"He remembered the greeting!" a third gasped.

I sat frozen, head down, wishing I could vanish.

But beside me, Sandy stretched his fingers and grinned. "Arre, not bad. Today's session was actually lighter than usual."

Sam rubbed his hands, whispering, "Mine are burning. But movie was worth it."

Piddu, with swollen palms, still managed a dramatic line: "Think positive, he only knows that we bunked his class, not the school yesterday."

I didn't laugh. I couldn't. My cheeks stung, my pride stung more.

And then, as I raised my head, I saw Gayatri looking back at me, her eyes were still wet. No anger, no mockery. Just a small nod, as if to say, *I stood by you, don't worry.*

That single look hit harder than all sixteen slaps.

Students rushed out for recess. But I stayed seated, my mind heavy, my cheeks still burning.

Gayatri walked up to me, pulled out a page from my notebook, scribbled, "Don't worry, keep smiling," and then gave me a warm smile.

It was the day I bunked school. The day I got caught. The day my pride was shattered.

That day, my cheeks burned, my pride sank, and my reputation as a "good boy" went into permanent damage. That day taught me that real friendship stands with you, even in shame.

Mission No Punishment

Our last adventure had ended in total disaster.... for me.

After the mess we'd landed in last time, Gayatri wasn't her usual talkative self. She looked half worried, half tired — like a teacher who's given up explaining the same thing for the tenth time.

She folded her arms, took a deep breath, and said,

"Enough, guys. You all really need to get serious. What happened in Chauhan sir's class was not acceptable. I challenge you all to survive one week without getting punished."

We froze. Even Sandy stopped mid-smile.

Sandy blinked. "One week? Without punishment?"

"Yeah," Gayatri said, voice steady. "Just a week. If you manage that, I'll admit you can behave like normal and matured human beings"

Now that was personal.

Piddu leaned back, "Challenge accepted."

He said it like some Bollywood hero accepting a fight scene.

Gayatri smiled slightly. "Let's see how long your bravery lasts. Maybe two periods?"

After class, the gang huddled at the neem tree adda like it was a war meeting.

Sandy was pacing, "Guys, we can do this. Just one week."

I said, "We can't. You can't stay quiet even for one minute."

"Arre, this time serious," Sandy said. "No talking, no jokes, no punishment. We'll show her."

Piddu added dramatically, "We'll be the symbol of discipline. From Monday, LLB stands for *Lords of Learning and Behaviour.*"

Everyone laughed.

I said, "Forget discipline, just make sure you don't laugh when the teacher says something funny."

We all nodded like soldiers ready for battle.

For one week, no punishment. No mischief. No fun.

It sounded simple.

But for our gang, it was like asking fish to live without water.

Still, the plan was on.

The challenge was real.

From Monday, No Punishment Week would begin.

And honestly, we had no idea what disaster-free life even looked like.

It was Monday morning, Sandy walked into class like a different person.

And when I say different, I mean *unrecognisable.*

His hair, usually flying in all directions like he had just come from a wind tunnel, was now soaked in coconut oil. It was shining so much, you could probably see your reflection in it.

He looked like a mixture of Amol Palekar from the 70s and a salesman.

The whole class went silent for two seconds, trying to process what we were seeing.

Then I whispered, "Bro… did you fall into an oil tank?"

Sandy gave a saintly smile, "Discipline, my friend. This is the new me."

I couldn't hold it anymore. "You look like you're going for a marriage proposal in 1978."

Even the teacher stopped mid-sentence when he walked in.

"Good morning, ma'am," Sandy said politely, joining his hands like some devotional TV serial actor.

The teacher stared for a moment. "Sandy… are you okay?"

"Yes, ma'am," he said, in his sweetest possible voice. "I'm just trying to be… sincere."

The teacher nodded slowly, clearly suspicious.

For the rest of the morning, Sandy sat perfectly straight, nodded during lectures, and even asked one or two *real questions.* The gang was in shock.

During lunch break, Gayatri came to our bench.

"So far, so good," she said. "No punishment yet."

Piddu was eating quietly. "I'm telling you, this Sandy will blow it before Thursday."

Sandy adjusted his hair and said proudly, "This Sandy 2.0 is born again. No jokes, no naughtiness."

I said, "Forget jokes, you should carry a mop. That oil can clean the whole classroom."

He ignored me, humming an old Kishore Kumar song like some retro hero.

But honestly, I had to admit, the transformation was working.

For once, Sandy looked *almost* innocent.

The gang was behaving. The teachers were relaxed.

That day, our classroom looked… strange.

No noise. No giggling. No paper balls flying across the room.

Usually, when the teacher walked in, our gang would be whispering, passing notes, or fighting over samosas. But today, everyone was sitting straight like statues in a wax museum.

The teacher entered, looked around, and froze.

"What happened to XII C?" she asked suspiciously.

Sandy stood up politely. "Good morning, ma'am."

She narrowed her eyes. "Are you people planning something?"

"No, ma'am," the entire class replied in one voice, like a chorus.

She stared at us for a moment longer, then slowly turned to the board. But you could tell, that she didn't trust it. None of the teachers did.

The silence continued period after period.

By lunch, the entire class had joined in our strange experiment. Everyone was quiet, pretending to be model students just to see how far it would go.

When the final bell rang, Gayatri whispered, "Day one done. No punishment."

We all grinned like freedom fighters after a successful protest.

But honestly, the silence was harder than we imagined.

It wasn't just about not getting punished, it was about not being *us.*

And that, for the LLB gang, was the biggest punishment of all.

By the third day, our so-called "No Punishment Week" had turned into a full-blown survival test.

Staying quiet was harder than any exam.

For a group that couldn't sit still for even five minutes, behaving was like fasting, your body can do it, but your soul starts screaming.

Sandy made a new rule:

"Speak only when absolutely necessary."

I asked, "Like when we're on fire?"

"Yes," Sandy said seriously. "Or if the teacher asks a direct question. Otherwise—zip."

So, we went through the day in silence.

Piddu was the worst.

He had this habit of sneezing like a lion. Once it started, it couldn't be stopped.

So when the sneeze came, he tried to hold it. His face turned red, his eyes watered, and he made this weird sound, something between a hiccup and a dying goat.

The teacher turned, "Are you okay, Piddu?"

He nodded quickly, tears rolling down.

We were dying inside, trying not to laugh.

Sandy passed a small note under the desk: *Control your engine, bro.*

Just then, the teacher spotted the paper.

For a moment, everything froze.

This was it, our perfect record was about to be destroyed.

She picked up the note, unfolded it… and smiled.

"Engine? What engine?" she asked.

We all stared blankly, pretending to be confused.

She sighed, shook her head, and continued teaching.

No punishment. We had survived again.

After the class, we celebrated silently, just eye contact and victory smiles.

It felt like winning a war without firing a shot.

But inside, the pressure was building.

We weren't made for this peaceful life.

Every joke we didn't crack was like a fire waiting to burst.

I whispered to Sandy, "Bro, this silence is more dangerous than the punishments."

He nodded, whispering back, "I know. But we're almost there. Just two more days."

Two more days, that's what he said.

But as everyone knows, in our gang's world, two more days is exactly when destiny starts preparing its next comedy show.

Saturday morning.

The final day of our "No Punishment Week."

The air in Class XII-C felt different, calm, careful, and a little bit tense. We had made it five days without trouble, and now only two periods stood between us and history.

Sandy walked in like a general inspecting his troops.

"Gentlemen," he said, "we've come too far to fall now. No jokes, no distractions. Today, we'll make Gayatri eat her words."

I whispered, "And after that, samosa party."

Piddu nodded, "Double samosa. No sharing."

The first two classes went surprisingly smoothly.

Everyone was alert. Sandy kept giving silent hand signals like a traffic cop every time someone even twitched.

At one point, a chalk piece fell from the teacher's hand, and the class collectively froze, because normally, that's when we'd start our commentary.

But today, not a sound

Even the teacher looked impressed.

By lunch, we could sense victory in the air.

Gayatri and Nidhi came to our bench, smiling like proud parents

"So… looks like you boys actually did it," Gayatri said.

"Of course," Sandy said proudly. "No punishment. Not even one."

Nidhi laughed, "I don't believe it. Check with every teacher once. Maybe they forgot to report you."

"Jealousy shall not win," Piddu declared dramatically, biting into his sandwich.

The final bell rang.

That moment, oh, what a moment.

We jumped, high-fived, shouted, and hugged like we had just won the World Cup.

Gayatri finally said, "Fine. You won. No punishment for one week. I'm impressed."

We grinned from ear to ear.

Sandy puffed his chest. "See? Told you. LLB gang is now rebranded, *Legends Living Better.*"

Everyone laughed.

The week was officially over.

We had survived silence, avoided chaos, and proved we could behave, at least when challenged.

But then came the best part.

Sandy looked at us and said, "Now that the challenge is done... celebration tonight at Piddu's house."

We all cheered.

By evening, we had all landed at Piddu's house, our chosen venue for the "Victory Party."

His parents were gone for a wedding, and we had exactly three hours before they returned. For our gang, that was more than enough time to make lifelong memories, and mild chaos.

Gayatri and Nidhi arrived a little later, pretending to act decent but clearly amused.

"So this is your celebration idea?" Gayatri asked, looking at the pile of chips and Frooti bottles on the table.

"Of course," Sandy said, opening a packet of Kurkure. "This is luxury, madam. Teenagers can't afford wine and cheese."

We all laughed and settled on the floor. Someone played music softly on a tape recorder.

For ten minutes, it actually looked like a calm, decent get-together.

Then Sandy stood up, with that *"watch me"* face.

He said, "Guys, I'm telling you, I'm not just disciplined now, I'm also mature."

I smirked, "Mature?

Sandy replied seriously. "I'm talking about being grown-up. Real men stuff."

We all looked at each other, suspicious and excited, that tone usually meant disaster.

Then Sandy pulled out a notebook from his bag.

And without saying a word, he tore a page.

"What are you doing?" I asked, already suspicious.

"Shhh," he whispered, looking around dramatically like a secret agent. "I'm making a cigarette."

Gayatri blinked. "What!"

Nidhi gasped. "Sandy, have you lost it?"

Sandy grinned like he'd just invented fire. "Relax, ladies. It's just paper. I'll show you how men smoke in movies."

He stuffed some dry tea leaves inside, because obviously, tobacco wasn't part of his stationery, rolled it tight, and licked the edge to seal it.

Then he struck a matchstick.

The flame flickered.

He lifted the "tea cigarette" to his lips.

And in that one puff, his entire expression changed.

His face went red. Then pink.

He coughed once. Then twice. Then his lungs basically applied for leave.

"Bro! You okay?" Piddu shouted, patting his back.

Sandy waved his hand, eyes watering, trying to look cool between coughs.

"See… this… is how… men… smoke," he wheezed, still pretending to exhale like a Bollywood hero in slow motion.

The smell of burnt paper and tea filled the air, like someone was making chai inside a photocopy machine.

That was it. We couldn't take it anymore. The whole gang burst out laughing.

Between coughs, Sandy said, "See… this is… experience!"

"Yeah," I said, laughing, "Experience of dying!"

He finally threw the paper away, gasping for air.

The house echoed with laughter, the kind you remember for years.

After the chaos settled, Sandy sat quietly, still red-faced.

But he smiled too. "Fine, fine. I accept defeat. Smoking is cancelled."

"Good," Gayatri said, still giggling. "Next time try yoga instead."

We all clapped sarcastically, cheered, and continued snacking.

For once, it felt like the perfect ending to a perfect week, until Piddu decided it was *his turn* to show his manhood.

And that, my friend, is when the real storm began.

After Sandy's "coughing experiment," peace returned for exactly five minutes.

Then Piddu, who had been quiet till now, stood up with that dangerous sparkle in his eyes.

"Okay," he said, "now it's my turn."

We all froze.

"Turn for what?" Gopal asked suspiciously.

Piddu smiled mysteriously. "To show my power."

Before we could stop him, he walked to the corner of the living room, bent down near the old wooden cupboard, and pulled out a half-hidden bottle wrapped in newspaper.

Sandy's eyes went wide. "Is that what I think it is?"

Piddu nodded proudly. "Yes. The secret treasure of my father, Old Monk."

The room fell silent for a second.

Even Gayatri looked shocked. "You've lost your mind. Your father will kill you if he finds out!"

Piddu brushed his hand dramatically through his hair. "Relax. I'll add water later. He won't know."

Sandy laughed nervously, "That's not how it works, genius!"

But Piddu was already on his mission.

He brought out a couple of steel glasses from the kitchen, poured the brown liquid carefully, and sniffed it like a professional.

Then he said, "Two pegs. That's it. For confidence."

We shouted together, "Don't do it!"

But of course, he did.

One peg, gone in a gulp. Second peg, straight after.

For a minute, nothing happened. He looked fine.

Then suddenly, his face changed.

Sandy asked, "You okay?"

Piddu smiled weakly. "Of course, bro. I am… *feeling powerful.*"

Ten seconds later, he wasn't powerful anymore.

He was *horizontal.*

He started burping, hiccupping, and making noises that sounded like an old diesel truck starting in winter.

We rushed to hold him as he stumbled around the room.

And then, it happened, the great eruption.

Piddu puked.

Not just a little, he puked like his body was launching everything it had ever stored

On the floor, near the sofa, then halfway to the bathroom.

Everything he'd ever eaten, school lunch, snacks, came out that evening.

Sandy shouted, "Bro! Control the pressure!"

We couldn't breathe from laughing.

Gayatri covered her face, saying, "Oh my God! This is disgusting!"

Nidhi was laughing so hard, tears were rolling down her cheeks.

It was chaos, the funniest, messiest chaos ever.

When Piddu finally sat down, pale and exhausted, he looked at us and whispered weakly,

"One day… **I'll prove my capacity**."

That was it.

We lost it again.

The whole house filled with laughter that just wouldn't stop.

Even Gayatri, trying to act serious, burst out laughing finally.

The night ended with everyone mopping, laughing, and swearing to never try anything "macho" again.

By the time we finished cleaning up, it was almost 9 p.m.

The smell of whiskey, laughter, and Dettol had mixed into one confusing perfume.

Piddu was lying on the sofa, looking like a soldier who had just returned from war.

Sandy sat next to him, patting his back, trying not to laugh again.

"Next time," Sandy said, "start with Limca, not liquor."

Piddu groaned, "Shut up, yaar… it was just… experimental."

I said, "Yeah, like your science projects that always exploded."

Gayatri rolled her eyes. "You boys are unbelievable."

But even she was smiling now.

We all sat there, tired, laughing, and munching the leftover chips.

Nidhi looked around and said softly, "You know, this was actually fun."

I nodded. "Yeah, no punishment, but full entertainment."

Sandy grinned, "See? We balanced it perfectly. Discipline outside, disaster inside."

Everyone laughed.

After a while, the music played softly again, that old cassette player struggling to keep the beat.

We sat in silence for a few moments, sipping Frooti and staring at the ceiling fan spinning lazily.

The house was peaceful now, but it carried the echo of our laughter, loud, free, and unforgettable.

Gayatri stood up to leave and said, "Okay, legends, it's time to go before Piddu's father comes home and gives *all* of us punishment."

We grabbed our bags and tiptoed out like thieves, giggling all the way to the gate.

Before leaving, Sandy turned to Piddu and said, "Next time, just celebrate with samosas, okay?"

Piddu raise his hand, "Next time, **I'll prove my Capacity**."

We all burst out laughing one last time.

As we walked down the quiet lane under the yellow streetlights, I remember thinking that somewhere between silence, laughter, and chaos, we ended up creating a memory that would stay forever.

We didn't win a trophy.

No teacher clapped for us.

Just a week without punishment, and a lifetime's worth of laughter.

— The First Great Mass Bunk —

Present Day- 2025

A sudden laugh escaped my mouth, out of nowhere.

It brought me back to the present.

For a moment, I wasn't even sure what made me smile, maybe Piddu's face right after he puked, or Sandy's helpless coughing fit.

I looked out of the window. The building across the street stood still in the night, its rows of windows glowing faintly. The lights from each flat were soft, tired, like people finishing another day.

They looked a lot like my school memories, still there, but fading a little more every year.

I brushed aside a few photos and saw something peeking out from the box, a small, half-torn slip of paper.

When I pulled it out, I realised what it was, a *Rangeela* movie ticket.

The print had almost vanished, but the name was still there in bold red letters, fighting age, **RANGEELA** along with a faint seat number: *Balcony A-12.*

I smiled the moment I saw it.

The paper was yellowed, fragile at the edges, and smelled faintly of old paper. Half the ticket was missing, maybe it just didn't survive time.

The theatre's name was barely visible now, but I didn't need it.

Rupam cinema.

Gone years ago.

Where now stood a glassy mall with an air-conditioned multiplex and coffee that costs more than our entire balcony ticket.

I still remember that morning.

School days- 1996

Morning at school started like any other.

Students were rushing into the classroom before the morning assembly. Everyone was busy chattering away, the whole scene looked no less than a fish market.

Then came the shock.

Our class teacher Sharma Sir stepped into the class room.

Everyone fell silent with surprise.

"Why he here now" students started whisper.

"Students…" His voice was heavy.

"I have sad news. Our Vice Principal madam, Mrs. Apte, passed away this morning."

It was pin-drop silence. You could even hear the pigeons flapping against the window.

Someone behind whispered, "What….? Really?"

"Yes" another muttered. "She was fighting cancer for months."

It hit us. Madam was only a few months away from retirement. Strict face, but soft heart. She had scolded us many times, but also saved us from bigger punishments.

Sharma sir continued, "School will remain open today, but there will be no regular classes . Teachers will attend the rituals. You all must remain in class for self-study, The Class monitor has to maintain discipline in the class."

Self-study? The word itself was a joke. You know how students react when they hear that. We exchanged looks. Within minutes, small whispers spread like wildfire across rows.

I turned and looked at Sandy. He already had that mischievous grin.

"Arre bhai, this kind of chance doesn't come again and again," he said.

Piddu added in a low voice, "Madam won't... you know... die again."

We glared at him. "Moron! Have some respect!"

He raised both hands. "Sorry sorry... I mean, we won't get this kind of chance again."

That cracked a few giggles, even though the situation was serious. Typical Piddu, wrong line at the wrong time.

Sam leaned back, resting both hands behind his head, and asked, 'So, what's the plan?

Sandy's eyes twinkled. "Movie. Latest blockbuster. *Rangeela*."

I almost dropped my jaw.

"Bunk? Are you serious?"

After the last episode, I had sworn never to bunk again . And now these idiots were talking about bunking like it was nothing.

"Arre, this isn't really bunking, my friend," Piddu said, putting his hand on my shoulder.

"Anyway, there's no study today. We'll just waste time here playing and gossiping. So why not step out and enjoy properly?"

For once, his logic actually made sense. I was still confused, but I couldn't argue.

Sandy clapped his hands. "You're coming, GEM. Don't worry."

"Yes... yes.... *Rangeela* " Piddu jumped in, eyes sparkling.

"I heard A.R. Rahman's music is killer," Sam added.

"I don't care about music," Piddu grinned, "all I know is Urmila... in micro minis." His imagination was already running faster than us.

"And I heard Rupam cinema just installed new imported Dolby speakers from the US, first of its kind in India just for this movie," Sandy declared proudly, like he was the one who carried them from customs.

Gayatri, sitting two rows away, overheard. She usually ignored these mad plans. But today she surprised us.

"If it's Rangeela, I'm in." she winked at me.

Nidhi nodded too. "Me also. Anyway, there's no study."

That sealed it. If the girls agreed, the plan had already succeeded.

News spread faster than exam timetable gossip. By the time assembly ended, nearly twenty students had joined the mass bunk mission. It wasn't just an LLB gang stunt anymore. This was a proper revolution.

We all gathered near the back corridor, the one with broken windows and a neem tree giving some shade. Sandy looked around like a general addressing his army.

"Alright, soldiers. Here's the plan."

Sam chuckled, "Bhai, stop acting like Subhash Chandra Bose. Just tell us how we're leaving."

Sandy smirked. "Backdoor. Simple. I've already managed peon kaka."

I raised an eyebrow. "Managed? What did you give him?"

Sandy puffed up with pride. "One samosa. Hot and crispy. One bundle of Ramgadh Bidi. The man melted."

Everyone burst out laughing. Trust Sandy to bribe his way with a samosa and bidi.

Sandy continued. "Listen, we go one by one. Not in groups. Too risky."

The girls stood slightly aside, listening quietly. Gayatri looked amused. Nidhi was already nervous, glancing at the corridor every few seconds.

"What if someone catches us?" she whispered.

Gayatri shrugged. "Relax, it's only the backdoor. Most of the teachers are at the funeral anyway.

Piddu, trying to sound brave, added, "And anyway, once we're twenty people together, who will dare stop us? We'll look like a school rally."

Sam snorted. "Yeah, except instead of banners we'll be carrying coin boxes for balcony tickets."

The thought of getting caught did scare us a little. But the thrill of doing something forbidden was stronger. Our hearts were already racing.

One by one, we slipped out through the backdoor. The peon stood there, pretending to dust the gate lock. When Sandy passed him, he whispered, "Kaka, remember, one samosa and bidi bundle more in evening."

The peon just grinned, chewing the last bite of his earlier bribe.

We were out.

With such a big group, we couldn't just hop into buses. Our passes were only valid for school–home routes and timings. Any bus conductor would catch us.

Sam did quick math. "Okay, walking it is. Rupam cinema, one hour by foot. If we start now, we'll make it before the noon show."

Everyone groaned but agreed. Twenty teenagers walking through dusty lanes, in school uniforms, trying to look casual but clearly up to something.

The gang had barely walked ten minutes before the first disaster struck.

Piddu, who had proudly announced the night before that he was "now a seasoned drinker," suddenly slowed down. His face turned pale.

Sam frowned. "Arre, what happened?"

Piddu clutched his stomach. "Feeling… something odd inside my stomach."

Within seconds, he bent over and puked near the gutter. A couple of crows, who were enjoying leftover vada pav, flew away in disgust, flapping like they were filing a complaint.

Sam, dead serious, asked, "Pregnant?"

The entire group exploded. Laughter echoed down the road.

"Shut up yaar!" Piddu snapped, wiping his mouth with a handkerchief that looked more dirtier than clean.

Sandy held his nose dramatically. "Woh… last night you had pegs again or what, which are still working, haan?"

"Arre shut up pal," Piddu muttered. "It's just the sun. Too harsh today."

Sam put his hand on Piddu's shoulder. "Yes, yes. Blame Surya devta. Don't blame whisky devta."

"Next time try milk instead of whiskey," Sandy teased.

He added, "Or Bournvita. At least you'll get strong bones."

The gang laughed again. Poor Piddu walked silently, holding his stomach, already regretting his overconfidence.

That set the tone. The walk to Rupam cinema was not going to be peaceful.

A little further, Sandy became the next victim. He was trying to act smart, imitating Aamir Khan's tapori walk from *Rangeela*, when destiny struck. His left foot landed right in the middle of a fresh cow dung pile.

Splaaat!

He slipped and fell sideways, his pants making a tearing sound so loud that everyone froze for a second. Then the laughter erupted like Diwali crackers.

"Arre wah!" Sam clapped. "Public performance, free of cost!"

Sandy stood up, inspecting the damage. The entire backside of his pants had split open.

Piddu giggled, "your 'Rangeela' just became 'Ang-leela' *(ang → bodypart in Hindi)* ."

Sandy's face turned red. "Shut up and find a solution! Otherwise I'll have to roam the whole day like this, full exposure... and I'm sure you idiots won't enjoy that view!"

Sam suggested tying his jacket around Sandy's waist, but the jacket was too small, more like a belt than a cover.

Finally, a roadside tailor, an old man in his 70s, noticed the commotion and came over. He inspected Sandy's pant, shook his head seriously like a doctor giving bad news.

"Son, this is badly torn from the middle. Zip also gone. I will try to repair, but it will take some time. Come to my shop" he said, stroking his moustache.

We all went to his shop. Old man looked around, lowered his voice, and whispered, "Problem is... I don't have any changing room here. Where will you hide till I fix it?"

Sandy looked desperate. "So what do I do? Stand here like a naked statue?"

The tailor thought for a second, then shrugged. "No worries. Take this bedsheet for temporary cover." He raised his hands and handed over a rolled-up cloth.

Sandy opened it and froze.

"Bedsheet?" he almost shouted. "That too with Disney cartoons printed on it?"

Everyone leaned in. Pluto the dog was smiling right in the middle of the sheet.

Before Sandy could react, Piddu doubled over laughing. "Take it, take it! Just be careful... if Pluto bites, the whole bedsheet will roll down and expose your future family planning department."

The entire group exploded. Some fell on the footpath, clutching their stomachs. Even Gayatri and Nidhi, who tried hard to stay composed, couldn't stop laughing.

Sandy's face turned red. He quickly wrapped the bedsheet around himself, muttering, "Shut up, all of you! Just pray no one from school sees me like this."

Sam smirked. "Don't worry. Even if they see, they'll think you joined some Disney fancy-dress competition."

The gang roared again as Sandy stomped ahead, Pluto wagging happily on his backside.

So, for the next twenty minutes, Sandy walked wrapped in a faded blue bedsheet like some half-saint, half-ghost. People stared.

We couldn't breathe from laughing.

"Careful Sandy," Sam said, "if you trip again, you'll be giving a full fashion show."

Meanwhile, the rest of the group kept themselves entertained. Piddu started singing *"aaye re aaye re, pant faad ke aaye re"* loudly, and soon everyone joined.

People on the road turned to look at this strange parade of uniform-clad students singing filmi songs while one of them was dressed like a wandering baba.

Gayatri grinned. "Actually, he is. Full pagal. But you know… these boys, for all their mischief, they're good at heart. And the way they stick together… it's something special."

Nidhi glanced at the noisy gang ahead, Piddu still teasing Sandy, Sam whistling *aaye re aaye re*, Sandy trying to walk seriously but laughing anyway.

"Yeah," she nodded softly, "their bond is different."

Gayatri smiled again. "That's why I don't mind joining them. Feels like we're part of something bigger."

Finally, the tailor took around 15–20 minutes to stitch it up. Sandy got back his pants… and along with it, his lost dignity

After all the masti and nonstop teasing, we continued our march. Within a few minutes, we reached the main market.

Piddu spotted a pakora stall. "Guys, let's eat. I'm feeling weak after… you know."

Sandy glared. "First you vomit, now you want pakoras? You're a walking disaster."

But the smell of hot pakoras was too tempting. Everyone pooled coins and bought one plate, passing it around like holy prasad.

The stall owner looked suspicious. "Such a big gang, and only one plate? What's this drama?"

Sam grinned, "Uncle, ek plate main khane se pyar badta hai.. giving pose like Amir Khan in Andaz Apna Apna"

The man shook his head, muttering something about "This generation," but served anyway.

After snacks, the march continued. Dusty roads, random jokes, nonstop teasing.

"Arre, where are you all going?" one random uncle asked.

Sandy instantly lied, "Special Disney land parade!"

We all laughed and walked faster before they asked more.

After almost an hour and a half of chaos, laughter, and Sandy's "Pluto bedsheet adventure," we finally reached Rupam Cinema. The huge red-and-yellow hoarding of *Rangeela* was shining above the gate. Aamir Khan with his tapori cap, Urmila in her bright mini-dress, Jackie Shroff looking broody, it was calling us like a magnet.

Other students were waiting for us at the cinema hall.

"Where were you all" one asked.

Sandy replied, "We were watching special Disney land parade!"

We all laughed. Others were confused.

The theatre already had a crowd buzzing outside. Ticket windows were packed, people shouting, "Bhaiya, do balcony! Ek stall! Jaldi karo!"

That smell of roasted peanuts, samosa oil, and cheap perfume hung in the air, every cinema in the 90s had that same desi aroma.

"Alright, plan time," Sandy announced, puffing up like he was leading a military operation. "We'll buy tickets in small groups. Less chance of suspicion."

Gayatri raised an eyebrow. "Suspicion? Bhai, this is a cinema hall, not a CBI office."

Still, we agreed. We split. LLB gang plus Gayatri and Nidhi together, others in pairs and trios.

I checked my pocket. Barely a few crumpled notes and coins. "God, I am short of money," I muttered.

Gayatri noticed. Without a word, she slipped some money into my hand. "Don't worry," she said softly.

I hesitated, but before I could say thanks, Nidhi leaned to her and whispered, "Shall I share too?"

Gayatri smiled. "Already done."

That quiet moment said a lot. The girls weren't just tagging along; they were part of the gang now.

Finally, tickets in hand, balcony, first row. We strutted inside like VIPs.

The theatre was jam-packed. Ceiling fans whirred uselessly against the heat of hundreds of bodies. Boys with whistles in their mouths, families with kids, groups of college students, it was a festival mood.

We settled into our seats, the old red cushions squeaking under us. Sandy adjusted himself like a king. "Balcony seat, boss. Full paisa vasool."

The lights dimmed. A hush fell. Then the opening notes hit—loud, fresh, unlike anything we had ever heard. A. R. Rahman's magic. The Dolby speakers thundered, the bass shaking our bones.

"Guysssss!" Sam shouted over the noise. "These imported speakers are blasting like rockets! What a sound, yaar!"

The screen burst alive with colours. The first big song rolled in.

And there she was—Urmila. Bright dress, toned figure, dancing like fire on screen. She looked sizzling hot. Boys screamed, someone in the back shouted, "I love you Urmila!"

Piddu leaned forward, eyes wide. "Boss, forget Dolby, forget balcony… THIS is the main attraction."

Gayatri rolled her eyes. "Idiot." But even she couldn't stop smiling at his honesty.

I turned to Piddu. His mouth was wide open, eyes fixed on the screen without a single blink. Honestly, I was sure even his mouth had started watering.

Dancers filled the screen, energy exploding. We couldn't stop tapping our feet. Half the hall started clapping in rhythm.

Then came Aamir Khan's entry, Munna. His first line, "10 ka 30, 10 ka 30?" delivered with that street-smart attitude.

The theatre erupted. Whistles, screams, coins flying in the air. *Cling cling cling!* One coin hit Sandy's shoulder, another grazed Piddu's head.

Instead of getting angry, both stood up, holding the coins like trophies. "Aamir deserves more coins.....!" Piddu shouted, and the gang roared with laughter.

Scene after scene, the film had us hooked. Munna's tapori slang, Jackie's brooding silence, Urmila's bubbly charm—it was the perfect masala.

During one emotional scene, Jackie looked longingly at Urmila, Rahman's soft tune playing in the background. The hall actually went quiet. Even our gang stopped their nonsense for a few minutes.

Then suddenly another peppy song started, and the hall was back to madness. People dancing in aisles, clapping, shouting. Sandy actually stood up and did Munna's dance step in the balcony row.

"Sit down, idiot!" Sam pulled him down, but by then half the row was laughing.

Sam leaned towards me. "Bro, I'm telling you. This film isn't just a hit. It's history."

And he was right. *Rangeela* wasn't just another movie—it felt fresh, alive, and new. The music, the colours, the way Aamir spoke—it was like someone had opened a window in the stuffy 90s Bollywood room.

The interval bell rang. We ran outside for cold drinks. Of course, with empty pockets, we could only afford two bottles for the whole gang. We passed them around, everyone taking small sips like they were drinking nectar.

"Arre careful, don't finish it in one go!" Piddu scolded Sam, who had gulped too much.

Back inside, the second half had even more energy. Munna's struggle, Jackie's heartbreak, Urmila's rise to stardom, it all pulled us in. When the climax came, the theatre was thunderous. Cheers, whistles, and people throwing more coins.

By the time the end credits rolled, we were drained but glowing. We had laughed, screamed, clapped, whistled, and even ducked flying coins. It wasn't just a movie, it was an event.

As we walked out, Sandy sighed dramatically. "Guys, this is life—fun, drama, dance… what else do we even need?"

Piddu raised his hand like a school kid. "Urmilaaaaa?

Everyone burst out laughing as we spilled onto the hot afternoon street, humming Rahman's tunes, still lost in the magic of *Rangeela*.

The movie had drained our energy.

"Guys, let's take an auto back, I can't walk to school again," Sam groaned, stretching his legs like a tired old man.

Gayatri shook her head. "We don't have much money left."

"Okay fine, let's take sharing auto," Sam said quickly, not ready to give up.

We squeezed into two autos, half sitting, half hanging, and got down near our regular bus stop. Surprisingly, we were earlier than our usual school dispersal time.

"Guys, forty-five minutes are left before school ends," Sam said, checking his watch. "We can't go home straight. Parents will ask questions."

That's when Piddu's eyes lit up. "Guys, let's eat something! We need to pass time anyway. Straight to home will be boring."

Sandy frowned, patting his empty pocket. "Eat? With what money? After those balcony tickets, I don't even have bus fare left."

"Chill," Piddu said, already pulling out coins. "Let's see how much we all have. Everyone contribute."

One by one, people emptied their pockets. A few coins, some crumpled notes, and bus pass cards that were useless right now. It looked like a sad charity box.

Piddu counted, proudly raising the total like he had struck gold. "See? Enough for some bites, let's go to Lolit palace!"

Sandy's eyes widened. "Are you mad? Lolit Palace is not a place to 'manage.' It's the palace where your money disappears faster than magic."

"Trust me," Piddu insisted, puffing up his chest. "We can pull it off."

And just like that, our tired feet turned towards Lolit Palace, not knowing that the real drama of the day was still waiting for us.

The gang groaned. Lolit Palace wasn't a five-star, but for us it was no less. Red sofas, shiny glass tables, and waiters in bow ties—it was out of our league most days. But Piddu's excitement was infectious.

We walked in. The waiter scanned us from top to bottom— sweaty students in half-wrinkled uniforms, still smelling of cinema samosas. He wasn't impressed.

Still, he handed the menu with fake politeness.

The girls solved the problem first. Gayatri looked at Nidhi and said, "One samosa. We'll share."

The waiter raised an eyebrow. "One samosa?" He scribbled slowly, like he was noting a crime.

The boys were worse. We stared at the menu like it was written in Greek. Everything looked expensive.

The waiter hovered, pen in hand. "Yes sir, what else?"

Awkward silence. Then, Piddu cleared his throat. "One soda."

The waiter blinked. "Just soda?"

"Yes. One soda."

The man didn't move, waiting for us to change the order. But Piddu nodded confidently, like he had planned it all. "One soda is enough."

We stared at him. Why just soda?

The waiter finally left, muttering under his breath. Two minutes later, one samosa and one soda arrived at our royal table.

As soon as the waiter walked off, Piddu grinned, unzipped his school bag, and pulled out a small bottle. Amber liquid shimmered inside.

Whiskey.

Our jaws dropped.

"Are you mad?" Sam whispered furiously. "This is Gujarat! Dry state! You want police to lock us up?"

"Relax," Piddu said, already pouring 60 ml into the glass. He grinned, "Just a while ago, you all were laughing at my *appetite* for drinking. Now watch properly, I'll show you what real capacity looks like."

"Remember guys, I told you that one day **I will prove my capacity**" He added

He topped it with soda, lifted the glass and gulped it in one go.

We looked around nervously. Some aunties were eating pav bhaji two tables away. A group of college guys sat near the window. The waiter was eyeing us suspiciously from the counter.

But Piddu leaned back, sighing loudly after his sip. "Ahhh! Now this is royal."

That sigh was his mistake. The waiter's ears perked. He walked straight to our table, picked up the glass, and sniffed. His eyebrows shot up.

He looked at us, then the glass again. "Whiskey?"

We froze. No one dared to speak.

"Come with me," he ordered, marching towards the manager's cabin.

Sam whispered, "Run."

In one motion, we left some coins and notes on the table, grabbed bags, and bolted. Chairs screeched, plates clattered. People stared as we stormed out like we were escaping a raid.

Except Sandy. He couldn't run. His bedsheet episode earlier had already slowed him down, and this time, his legs betrayed him again.

The manager grabbed his shoulder. "Stop! You guys were drinking Whiskey?"

Sandy stammered, sweat dripping down. "Not me … did you *see* me drinking?"

The manager hesitated.

"No, right? Then how can you blame me?" Sandy added, somehow steadying his voice.

The manager squinted, muttered something, and finally released him.

Sandy walked out fast, face pale. We were waiting outside, breathless.

"Run, guys, I'm also scared!" he said, almost crying.

We burst out laughing. For a moment, Sandy looked like a hero who had bravely faced the manager. But deep down, he was as terrified as the rest of us.

We waited for a while, hiding near Lolit Palace. Nothing moved, no one followed us. Everything looked normal again.

"Thank God… looks like the manager isn't taking this any further," Gayatri whispered.

We sat there quietly for the next fifteen minutes, letting the tension fade. Then, one by one, we caught our usual buses back home.

Next morning, we walked into school like nothing had happened.

It was last period before the lunch break. Bhatia madam stood near the blackboard, chalk in hand, explaining the law of demand. The class was unusually quiet.

Then the door creaked open.

The peon stepped in, followed by a man in plain clothes and a police constable.

Pin-drop silence.

Our hearts froze. Even the ceiling fan seemed to stop for a second.

Madam Bhatia frowned. "Yes?"

The peon bent and whispered something in her ear. She nodded gravely, then said, "Let them search."

The man stepped forward and stood near her desk. He crossed his arms, scanning the class like a detective in a crime movie. The constable loomed behind him, baton in hand.

My throat went dry. This was it. The restaurant manager must have sent someone. We were finished.

Piddu immediately ducked behind Ashu. "Oye, don't move, let me hide behind you," he hissed.

Ashu looked shocked. "Arre, what nonsense! Why are you sticking to me?"

"Just shut up! You're broader than me. Cover my face."

My stomach was twisting into knots.

The man began walking slowly, row by row, scanning faces. His eyes lingered on each of us for a second too long. Every step he took, our heartbeat doubled.

He reached near Piddu's row.

Piddu stiffened, staring at the ceiling as if he had never sinned in his life. Sweat dripped down his forehead. His lips moved in silent prayer.

The man stopped. Looked at him. Tilted his head.

We held our breath.

Then, just as suddenly, he moved on. Walked back to the front, leaned towards Bhatia madam, and whispered something.

Bhatia madam's sharp eyes scanned the class once, and then she nodded. The man and the constable left quietly.

The door closed.

For a moment, no one moved. Then a collective sigh of relief swept across the room.

The bell rang. Bhatia madam left the classroom.

Piddu grabbed his bag. "Bas, I'm done. I'm going home. Police came for me, I know it."

Other gang members also followed him to stop him.

We gathered under our favourite neem tree adda as fast as possible. Everyone was still shaken.

Piddu's voice was trembling. "That was the restaurant man. I'm telling you, he came to identify us. I was this close to going behind bars."

I shook my head. "Relax. I checked with the Peon kaka in the corridor. That man was from another restaurant. Some guys in school uniform had a fight there yesterday and smashed a few chairs. They came looking for them, not us. It seems they were from another school."

Silence for few seconds.

Then, all at once, the gang burst out laughing.

Sam slapped Piddu's back. "Arre, you nearly wet your pants for nothing!"

Sandy added, "And you wanted to show drinking *appetite* yesterday? Today you showed police-fearing capacity!"

Even Gayatri and Nidhi laughed openly. Poor Piddu hid his face, shaking his head, but a small smile crept in too.

The scare was over. The laughter was back. And for LLB gang, that balance—panic one moment, comedy the next—was life.

Annual Cultural Day – 'The Day of Drama'

Present Day- 2025

My mobile rang.

"Hello," I said, picking it up without even checking the screen.

"Bro, we all are starting now… will take another forty-five minutes to reach here," someone said over the call, his voice full of background noise and excitement.

"Yes bro, we're eagerly waiting for you guys. Come fast," I replied, smiling, and hung up.

I reached into the box again and pulled out two old photographs stuck together at the corners.

The first one made me smile instantly.

It was from our school's Annual Cultural Day, a group photo of students, including the LLB gang, standing on the stage, all dressed up in Punjabi attire, *Kurtas and Tambas*, and Gayatri and Nidhi in their colourful salwars.

None of us were posing with polite smiles for the camera, we were laughing out loud, caught in the middle of something ridiculously funny that had just happened.

Just looking at it made me laugh out loud, the same unfiltered laugh that had echoed across that dusty school ground years ago.

For a moment, I could hear it all again, "Tunak Tunak Tun" beats, the crowd cheering "Red Panther'.

I shook my head, still grinning, and wiped a tiny tear from the corner of my eye, the good kind of tear that comes with happy memories.

Then I picked up the second photo. It was from our Lonavala picnic.

The colours had faded, but I could still see it clearly, me and Gayatri sitting on a rock, facing the sunset.

And suddenly, my smile disappeared.

The laughter that had just filled my chest felt far away now.

All that remained was a strange stillness, the kind that comes when you remember something you can't go back to.

I looked at that photo for a long time.

I placed the picture back gently, my fingers lingering on it for a second longer than needed.

Some memories make you laugh and some make you quiet.

School days- 1996

More than half of our Class XII term was gone. The pressure of exams was there, but the festive season brought a strange kind of energy to the whole school.

Teachers were already whispering about the upcoming Annual Cultural Event, the grandest show of the year.

The announcement finally came during morning assembly.

"Students," Principal madam spoke from the stage with her usual serious face, "our annual cultural function will be held in fifteen days. I expect enthusiastic participation."

Annual cultural event always meant only one thing, full dhamal. Songs, dance, music, noise… everything packed in one stage. And the best part? You could bunk classes proudly, without even hiding. Just say "practice hai" and walk out of the class.

The crowd roared. Some clapped, some hooted, one fellow even shouted "Bolo Ambe maat ki... Jai" for no reason.

After assembly, classrooms buzzed like a vegetable market. Students were already planning who would sing, who would dance, and who would just sit in the audience and eat samosas.

That's when Kabir entered our story.

Kabir was from XII-A, science stream. He had joined only this year only. His father was in the Army, officer rank. Tall, broad shoulders, perfect hair, the kind of guy who looked like he was born ready for a commercial ads. In just a few months, he had built a reputation, good in studies, good in sports, and yes, girls noticed him too.

We were sitting in our classroom, half-discussing whether to participate or not, when Kabir walked in alongwith his classmates. He looked straight at us.

"Boys, I need your help," he said.

Piddu immediately replied, "Help? Sorry, bro. If it's about Biology homework, ask Sandy, he watches lot of movies with all kinds of open bodies."

Kabir laughed lightly. "Not homework. I want you all in my group for the Punjabi folk dance."

There was a silence. Then Sam almost choked on his water bottle.

"Punjabi dance? Us? Have you seen Gopal try to clap in rhythm? Forget bhangra, he can't even clap properly."

I gave Sam a look. "Thanks for the confidence boost."

Ashu leaned back in his chair. "Listen, Kabir. We don't do dance. Last time we tried, Piddu kicked the blackboard."

Everyone laughed, except Kabir. He was serious.

"I'm making a solid team. Need some crazy ones in it. And you people are already famous for that! This kind of performance needs dhamaka, not perfection. So come on, join in"

Piddu raised his hand like he was in court. "Excuse me, my dance has side effects. Last time I tried, my neighbour's TV stopped working."

Kabir shook his head, smiling patiently. "Don't worry. We'll practice. Dubey sir will help. You just need to show spirit."

Sandy muttered, "I'll perform only if there's a samosa-eating competition."

Kabir didn't give up. He started convincing each one. "Gopal, you are tall, you'll look good in the front. Ashu, you're fast with steps, you can handle centre moves. Sam, you're strong, you can do lifts, Piddu I have something special for you."

Sam frowned. "Lifts? I'm not carrying anyone."

"Not carrying," Kabir explained, "just some traditional bhangra steps. Easy."

We were still not convinced. Finally, Kabir pulled out his secret weapon.

"Gayatri you are also helping us. She'll be critic, watching practice and guiding."

"Me…!! How did I get dragged into this now?" Gayatri's eyes went wide.

Kabir leaned forward with his trademark confident smile. "Yes, Gayatri. You're Punjabi, so you already know the traditional steps. You can easily guide us if we go wrong anywhere."

She folded her arms. "That doesn't automatically make me a dance teacher."

Piddu whispered, "Gayatri? Watching every day?"

I could see Sam's ears turning red. Ashu was suddenly scratching his chin like he was thinking deeply. Even I was trying to hide a smile.

Kabir looked around, saw the hesitation breaking, and added, "So… are you all in?"

Piddu gave up first. "Alright, I'm in. But when people faint, don't blame me."

Sam sighed. "Fine… but if I go viral for the wrong reasons, you're explaining it to my parents."

Ashu nodded reluctantly. "Count me in. But I'm not wearing tight clothes."

Everyone looked at me.

"He's in too!" Gayatri declared, grabbing my right hand and raising it like I had just won an Olympic medal.

"Yeeaahhh!" we all screamed, clapping and whistling like mad.

Even Piddu stood up and started bowing like some chief guest.

Kabir's smile widened. Mission accomplished.

"Guys, we don't have much time. Tomorrow evening, cultural hall, attendance compulsory!" Kabir announced, then walked out with his classmates, leaving us staring like we had just joined NCC.

What we didn't realise at that time was this: his main goal was never really the dance. His main goal was something else.

Our very first practice day felt like punishment more than preparation.

After school, the whole campus looked like a mela. Everywhere you turned, some group was running for practice. Singing groups were carrying their harmoniums, drama kids were shouting random dialogues in the corridor, and the rangoli committee was already fighting over colours.

We dragged ourselves towards the cultural hall. Kabir was already there, standing tall like a team captain. With him were three of his classmates, Dinesh, Shantanu, and Rishi. They looked charged up, already stretching and warming up like Olympic athletes.

Sam whispered, "Dude, are we here for dance practice or sports day?"

We laughed, but deep inside we all knew, that was going to be serious business.

Dubey sir was already waiting, hands on his waist like some Bollywood choreographer.

"Dubey sir clapped his hands dramatically.

"Arre wah, Punjabi folk dance group!" he grinned. "Listen, boys… dance is never just about steps. It's about *feelings, emotions, connection.* You don't just do bhangra, you become the DHOL!"

Sam muttered from the back, "DHOL…!!!! If I become the dhol, someone will start beating me with sticks."

The gang burst out laughing.

Dubey sir clapped his hands loudly. "Okay, total eight people! Let's begin."

He adjusted his kurta like some TV choreographer and pointed at us. "Guys, I've already lined up four–five songs for the routine. We'll go step by step, song by song. First, I'll show you some basic moves. Just follow me."

He took position in the centre and gave a signal to start the music.

And there it was, the hall shook with one of the most energetic tracks of Daler Mehndi: "Tunak Tunak Tun."

Everyone shouted in excitement. Piddu even whistled so loudly that the echo bounced off the walls.

The entire hall instantly filled with an electric vibe, like some mini rock concert was about to start.

Dubey sir started with some easy steps. Hands up, shoulders bouncing, legs moving in rhythm. He danced so smoothly that for a moment we forgot he wasn't even Punjabi.

Sam whispered, "Bhai, if Dubey sir opens a dance academy, half the Punjabis will be out of business."

We burst out laughing, while sir kept grooving like he was auditioning for the MTV show.

"Stop the music!" Dubey sir shouted, raising his hand like a film director. The hall went quiet.

"Now it's your turn to try these steps," he announced, breathing heavily but smiling like a rockstar.

We all clapped loudly for his performance.

Piddu muttered, "Sir, if we clap enough, maybe he'll keep dancing and forget about us."

Ashu elbowed him, but we couldn't stop laughing.

"Take positions as mentioned in this paper," Dubey sir said, pulling out a folded sheet from his pocket like it was a secret war plan.

We all gathered around.

"He actually made a pyramid formation… with our names written in boxes!" Ashu raised his eyebrows. "That's impressive. Feels like we're going for Republic Day parade, not dance practice."

Sam laughed, "Next he'll bring a science model and explain bhangra with Newton's laws."

We laughed, while Dubey sir stood proudly, as if unveiling a masterpiece.

Kabir stood in the centre, chest out, already moving like a pro. He looked at Gayatri, who was sitting on a chair nearby with her notebook, acting like a judge from some reality show.

"Gayatri, watch carefully," Kabir said, smiling. "Tell us where we go wrong."

"Don't worry," she replied. "I'm sure you'll give me plenty of mistakes to note down."

Piddu stepped forward, tried the basic move, and ended up facing the wrong direction. Everyone else was facing front, and Piddu was smiling proudly at the back wall.

Dubey sir stopped the music. "Pradeep, audience will be in front, not on the wall. Unless you are planning to impress lizards."

The hall burst out laughing.

We started again. Kabir, as expected, was sharp. He moved with full energy, shoulders bouncing, feet landing perfectly. Ashu was also decent, picking up steps quickly. I was struggling a bit, but at least I looked human.

Piddu, however…

He jumped half a second late, landed two steps away from his spot, and then suddenly invented some random move that looked like Bharatnatyam mixed with Bhangra.

Sam shouted, "Piddu, this is bhangra, not a martial arts movie!"

Everyone cracked up, even Gayatri.

For the next one hour, practice looked less like dance and more like a Piddu comedy show.

Every time we tried a step, he either went left instead of right, or jumped so late that it looked like he was dancing in slow motion. By the end of the hour, we had managed only half the first song.

"Okay guys, let's take a ten-minute break," Dubey sir announced, clapping his hands.

We all collapsed on the floor near Gayatri, panting and dripping with sweat like we had just run a marathon.

Piddu lay flat on his back and groaned, "This is not dance… it's punishment."

Gayatri laughed, shaking her head.

Kabir proudly pulled out a Five Star from his pocket and held it out. "For the judge," he said, giving his best hero smile.

"Thanks for this," Gayatri replied. She unwrapped it, broke off a tiny piece, and then, without thinking twice, passed the rest to me.

"He loves Five Star more than his life," she said, smiling.

I grabbed it happily while the gang started laughing.

Piddu clapped. "Wah Kabir! You wanted to impress Gayatri, and Gopal ended up with the chocolate."

Kabir forced a laugh, but his eyes told another story.

Later, Kabir tried again. "Gayatri, why don't you join for one step? It'll be easier to show them with you."

She shook her head firmly. "No way. I can't dance on this kind of songs, full of energy."

"Let's resume" Dubey sir came from outside, I guess after the smoke break.

For the next half an hour, we somehow dragged ourselves through the remaining half of the song.

I was struggling badly with one step. Even after trying three–four times, my shoulder bounce looked like a broken ceiling fan. Finally, I tripped and almost fell flat.

Before I could recover, Gayatri jumped up from her chair. "Don't worry, Gopal. Let me show you slowly." She stood beside me, clapping in rhythm, guiding me step by step until I got it right.

The gang clapped and whistled. I smiled in relief.

But Kabir's smile vanished faster than samosas vanish when Sandy is around.

We continued the practice for next half an hour.

By the end of that two hour, our legs were crying. Dubey sir declared, "Good start. But Pradeep, beta, your dance is moving in Richter scale, not rhythm scale."

Everyone laughed again, except poor Piddu, who looked like he was about to faint.

As we walked out of the hall, Gayatri closed her notebook. "Don't worry, boys. You'll improve. And Kabir, good idea. This group has potential."

Kabir's face lit up. Mission Gayatri was slowly working.

We all dragged ourselves towards the exit of the hall, none of us able to walk in a straight line. It looked less like a dance group going home and more like patients returning from physiotherapy.

Piddu groaned, "If this is just practice, the real performance will need stretchers."

We all laughed and start walking towards the bus stop.

The cultural event was now just two days away.

That meant this was our final rehearsal.

By the time we entered the hall, all of us looked serious for the first time in weeks. Even Sam, who usually cracked jokes, was warming up like he was about to play a cricket match.

Dubey sir clapped his hands. "Okay, boys, this is the last chance. So today, Full energy!"

We nodded like obedient soldiers.

But Piddu looked the most nervous. He kept tying and re-tying his tamba belt every two minutes.

Ashu teased, "Arre, why so much practice with tamba? Planning to model for men's fashion show?"

Piddu glared. "You people don't understand. If this belt opens on stage, my whole family will shift to another city."

The gang laughed, but inside we were also scared for him. After all, his somersault was the grand ending of the dance. If he failed, the whole performance would collapse like a card house.

We started with the first song. Steps were better now, almost in sync. Even I managed my shoulder bounce without tripping. Kabir, as usual, was sharp and full of energy. He kept throwing proud looks at Gayatri, who was sitting with her notebook, pretending to judge but mostly smiling at our madness.

Midway, the music stopped because Piddu jumped off-beat and crashed into the speaker wire.

Dubey sir held his head. "Beta, please, tomorrow if you break speaker, Principal madam will break me."

Gayatri tried to calm things down. "Don't worry. It's okay. You all are doing good."

Then she looked at me. "Especially you, Gopal. Much better now."

I smiled awkwardly. Kabir's face tightened again, though he quickly pretended to fix his kurta.

Finally, it was time for the closing move. The big somersault.

"Ready, Piddu?" Dubey sir asked.

Piddu stood in position, sweating like he had just run a marathon. He muttered, "If I die, tell my parents I went as a hero."

We all burst out laughing.

He ran, jumped, and flipped… and landed perfectly.

"Wah!" Dubey sir clapped. "That's it! Perfect! Just do the same tomorrow."

Piddu raised both hands like a champion. "See, told you. I'm a natural."

Sam smirked. "Natural disaster maybe."

The hall echoed with our laughter. For the first time, we actually felt ready. Nervous, yes… but ready.

And somewhere in that laughter, we realised, tomorrow, the real fun would begin.

The day had finally arrived.

Our annual cultural event.

The whole school looked like it was dressed up for a wedding. Rangoli at the entrance, lights hanging from windows, loudspeakers blasting with songs. Teachers were arriving in their best silk sarees and shiny blazers. Some students were running around like wedding planners.

We sneaked towards the backstage area, holding our costumes in plastic bags.

Inside, it was full chaos. Drama kids were screaming their dialogues, music group was tuning harmonium for the tenth time, and some junior was crying because his moustache for the play had fallen off.

Amidst all this, we found a corner to change into our Punjabi attire, kurta and tamba.

Sam looked at Piddu and said, "Oye, tie your belt tight, haan. If that tamba falls, audience will see bonus performance for free."

Ashu added, "And remember, no shorts inside. Dubey sir said it restricts the steps."

Piddu's face went pale. "Guys, fati padi hai? Why you all are after my tamba?"

Sam grinned, "You're the only one who gives bonus show without tickets."

We laughed, while poor Piddu kept re-tying his tamba like it was a matter of national security.

Once we were ready, we looked at each other. For the first time, the gang actually looked… good. The bright turbans, the colourful tambas, the glittering kurtas.

"Arre wah," Ashu said, striking a pose. "We look like a marriage dance party."

Sam added, "Yeah, except this time no one is serving paneer tikka."

We burst out laughing, which helped ease the nervousness.

Then Kabir walked in. And honestly, he looked like some Punjabi film hero straight out of a poster. The kurta fit him perfectly, the turban sat like a crown, and his broad shoulders did the rest.

"Wah Kabir," Piddu whistled, "if nothing works, at least you'll get a role in 'Khamoshi-2'"

Kabir just smiled and ignored the comment, his eyes already searching for someone.

And right on cue, Gayatri walked backstage. She looked elegant in her salwar suit, carrying a little notebook.

"Best of luck, boys," she said warmly, shaking hands with each one of us.

Sam blushed so much we thought he'd faint. Ashu gave a dramatic "thank you" bow. I smiled and nodded.

When she came to Kabir, he extended his hand too… but instead of just a handshake, he pulled her into a side hug.

Gayatri froze for a second, looking confused. She didn't react much, just smiled awkwardly and stepped back. But the gang noticed everything.

Ashu whispered in my ear, "Arre yaar, Kabir is playing Bollywood hero backstage only."

We chuckled silently, trying not to make it obvious.

Meanwhile, the program had already started. From backstage, we could hear the anchor shouting into the mic, "Ladies and gentlemen, welcome to our annual cultural function!"

Ganesh Vandana was performed first, followed by the principal's speech. The chief guest was already looking bored, but students cheered for every performance.

One by one, groups went up. Singing group got whistles, drama kids made everyone laugh, and the rangoli committee kept dragging every teacher to see their artwork.

Finally, the announcement came:

"Now, presenting the grand finale performance, Punjabi Folk Dance by Class XII!"

Our stomachs dropped. This was it.

Gayatri gave each of us a quick handshake again. "All the best, boys. You'll rock it."

We smiled nervously.

Kabir got ready like a commander leading troops to battle.

"Boys, this is it," Kabir whispered, puffing his chest. "Energy, coordination, confidence."

"Also tamba security," Sam muttered, tightening his knot one last time.

And just like that, we stepped towards the stage, hearts racing, tambas tied, and laughter hiding behind fear.

We lined up and the curtain opened.

The crowd roared. Some clapped, some hooted, and a few whistled so loudly, principal madam frowned on stage.

Music started, "Tunak Tunak Tun."

Kabir led in the centre, shoulders bouncing with perfect rhythm. Ashu nailed his steps. I followed carefully, hoping not to trip.

Then there was Piddu.

He began with the wrong hand, went left instead of right, and ended up facing the wings while the rest of us faced the crowd.

From the audience, someone shouted, "Oye, who's dancing with the wall?"

The hall burst out laughing.

Dubey sir, standing in the corner, buried his face in his hands.

Still, we pushed on. The second song kicked in, dhol beats growing louder. Kabir moved like a true Punjabi hero, tossing proud looks at Gayatri sitting in the front row. She clapped and cheered.

But Piddu… he was now one step behind everyone. When we raised one arm, he raised both. When we stomped, he jumped. By the third beat, he looked like he was auditioning for a karate movie.

Sam hissed, "Piddu! Not Bharatnatyam....Bhangra.... Bhangra!"

Piddu panicked, sped up, and almost collided into me. I pushed him back into line while the audience roared with laughter again.

Despite all this, the energy was electric. The crowd was clapping to the beat, hooting, cheering. Kabir kept smiling like a superstar.

Then came the grand finale moment, Piddu's somersault.

All eyes turned to him. He was sweating like a leaking water bottle.

In nervousness, instead of taking position in the centre, he kept stepping backward… and backward… until he was almost standing against the tall mike stand placed at the edge of the stage.

I whispered, "Arre, why is he reversing like a truck?"

"Shhh," Sam hissed, "let him focus."

Piddu bent down, adjusted his tamba, muttered something like a prayer, and ran forward, leapt, and flipped.

And… miracle of miracles… he nailed it. A perfect somersault.

We cheered, the crowd clapped, even Dubey sir threw his hands up in relief.

Piddu stood proudly, chest out, arms raised high like he had just won Olympics.

Piddu shouted, "Yahoo....., I'm champ!" and started running across the stage, both hands in the air.

But suddenly the crowd went silent. Only music was playing.

Piddu was still running from one corner to other corner of the stage.

That's when someone from the audience yelled, "Oye Piddu, look down!"

He looked down…

And the world went silent. Even the dhol beat felt like it paused in shock.

Tamba was missing.

For two seconds, Piddu stood frozen like a statue in some museum. Then he shouted, voice cracking through the hall,

"Arreeee! Where is my tamba?!"

It had got stuck on the stage mike during the flip, and there he was, running proudly across stage in his bright RED underwear.

The hall exploded. Laughter, whistles, stomping. Even the teachers couldn't hold it in. Principal madam hid her face with the program sheet. Smiling, the chief guest said into the mic, "Such dedication! Even costume can't stop him."

That made the hall even louder.

Meanwhile, poor Piddu rushed towards the mike stand, desperately trying to free his tamba. But the cloth was tangled in wires.

In full frustration, he shouted, "*Aaja you Bh*****!*" into the live mic. His voice echoed across the hall like a national announcement.

The audience was rolling on the floor. Some juniors fell off their chairs laughing.

Finally, Piddu managed to yank the tamba free, wrapped it around himself, and tried to run backstage. But the wire caught his foot and he fell flat on the stage.

But instead of standing up, in panic he started rushing forward on all fours, hands and legs scrambling on the stage floor like a wild animal escaping from the zoo.

The hall went mad. Someone shouted, "Arre look, Panther!"

Another voice corrected, "Panther? No no, *Red Panther!*"

The music was still playing, but nobody heard it over the laughter and whistles.

Sam muttered under his breath, "Forget bhangra, he just invented new dance, *Underwear Bhangra*."

Gayatri covered her mouth, but even she couldn't stop laughing.

And just like that, Piddu earned a new name in school history.

When the music finally ended and the curtain fell, the audience gave us the loudest applause of the night.

Not for the dance. For Red Panther's stunt.

Backstage, we collapsed on the floor, half-laughing, half-crying.

Dubey sir shook his head. "Beta Piddu… I choreographed a bhangra. You turned it into a circus."

Piddu sat quietly, face redder than his underwear.

Sam patted his back. "Cheer up. Today, you didn't just dance. You became a legend, you are now Red Panther."

We all kept laughing nonstop for the next ten minutes. Every time one of us tried to stop, someone would whisper, *"Red Panther,"* and the whole gang would burst out again.

Even Dubey sir was half-smiling, though he tried to act strict. Poor Piddu sat in the corner with his face buried in a towel, praying the ground would open up and swallow him.

By the time the event completely ended, the whole school was buzzing with one name: Red Panther. Juniors were chanting it in the corridors, teachers were whispering it with suppressed smiles, and even the chief guest left muttering, "Such… spirit."

That evening, Kabir called us all to Krishna Samosa Centre.

“My treat,” he said. “For our *successful* performance.”

We sat around the big steel table, samosas and chutney plates scattered everywhere. The laughter started again.

Ashu raised his glass of Thums Up. “Boys, a toast, to Red Panther!”

Everyone clapped, and Piddu hid his face behind a samosa.

“Arre, look at the bright side...no no RED bright side,” Sam added. “At least you got the loudest applause of the night.”

“Yeah,” I grinned, “and the only standing ovation for underwear Bhangra.”

The gang erupted again, banging the table till the shop owner glared at us.

Piddu groaned, “One day you all will die laughing, and I won’t even attend your funerals.”

But even he was smiling now, unable to resist the madness.

Somewhere between the laughter and samosas, we noticed Kabir and Gayatri sitting side by side, talking softly. For the first time, she seemed genuinely curious about Kabir, nodding and laughing at his stories.

Ashu whispered to me, “Arre, forget Piddu’s red panther act. Real story is starting here.”

I shrugged. “Could be… but today’s hero is only Red Panther.”

I grinned, dipping the samosa in chutney.

That night ended with samosa crumbs, sticky fingers, and sore throats from too much laughter. But one thing was clear, our gang had created history.

The performance would be forgotten in a week. But Red Panther? That name was carved forever in our school’s legend book.

— That Unforgettable Picnic —

After assembly we all came back and settled in class. It was Sharma Sir's accountancy period, so half of us were already bored before he even entered.

The door creaked, and in walked Sharma Sir, holding a piece of paper.

We stood up in chorus, "Good morning, sir."

He nodded, "Good morning. Students, I have to make an announcement."

The moment he said the word *announcement*, the whole class got alert. Normally his announcements meant surprise tests, sudden submissions, or some boring lecture about discipline. But today… he had that small smile on his face.

"Don't worry, you all will be excited after hearing this, So dates of this year's picnic are out now—"

Before he could even finish, the classroom burst like firecrackers. Everyone clapped, banged the desks.

Sharma Sir raised his voice over the chaos, "It's three days, two nights. Venue: Lonavala. Fees: Rs. 2500 per student. Fees to be paid by next week."

The cheering doubled. Some students started shouting "Lonavalaaa!" like cricket fans. The whole classroom turned into a fish market.

Piddu leaned over to me, whispering, "Bro, full three days of freedom. Just imagine, dance, masti, no parents, no Sharma Sir."

I laughed, "Sharma Sir will also come with us only. Apply break to your dreams and come back from Goa vibes."

Meanwhile, the murmurs were flying around:

“Arre I’m bringing Bluetooth speaker.” “I can bring the camera.”

“Will do tracking, it would be fun.”

Everyone was already planning like it was their personal wedding.

But while others were busy calculating snacks, I was stuck calculating something else Rs. 2500.

For many of my classmates, it was just a number. For me, it was a full month’s grocery bill. Asking Dad for that much, and that too just for picnic, made me uneasy.

I looked around at everyone’s excitement, with a forced smile but Gayatri caught me. She was like CCTV camera, always catching the smallest signal.

She leaned towards me and asked softly, “What happened? You don’t look happy. Picnic announcement and you’re sitting like someone failed you in prelims.”

I kept my forced smile intact, “Nothing, nothing. Just… thinking.”

Her eyes narrowed, “Thinking or worrying?”

I hesitated. She whispered again, “It’s the fees, right?”

I looked at her in surprise. How did she always guess?

Before I could reply, she said firmly, “If it’s about money, don’t even stress. I’ll manage.”

I muttered, “I can’t do that, Gayatri. It won’t feel right.”

She looked straight at me, “And it doesn’t feel right to see you skip picnic. If needed, I’ll pay. Simple.”

I chuckled, “Now you sound like EMI collector.”

She shot back, “And you sound like default customer. Just agree you’ll come.”

Her tone left no room for argument.

Meanwhile, news spread across divisions: not just our class, but all of XII A, B, C, and D were going.

LLB gang including Gayatri and Nidhi decided to join, calling it their "last ride together." The buzz doubled.

The first half of the day was spent only in picnic talks and wild planning.

Kabir had begun appearing in our class during lunch. He began showing up in our class at lunch. After Annual Day, he was suddenly a regular, and by now we understood the reason, he wanted to get closer to us.

"So… you all are coming for picnic, right?" he asked casually, but his eyes were never really on us. They were always on Gayatri.

Sandy leaned close and whispered in my ear, "Oh ho, Kabir bro suddenly became our best friend."

I just smiled.

Piddu added with his usual drama, "Haan, we were waiting only. Someone should come and ask us… then we'll all say yes together!"

The whole group burst out laughing.

But deep down, I had a strange feeling this picnic was going to be more than just masti.

Finally, picnic day arrived.

I somehow managed to arrange the fees, with some help from Dad, from cousins, and little from my own small savings.

I knew Dad had given money without saying a word, but I was sure he must have compromised on something to make it possible for me.

We were all very excited about this trip.

By evening 7 PM, the mandated time by Sharma sir to assemble, we all gathered near school with our bags.

The ground looked like railway platform, parents giving last-minute instructions, students dragging heavy bags, teachers trying to control the noise.

Sandy came late as usual, panting and carrying one huge suitcase.

Ashu teased, "Are you shifting house or coming for picnic?"

Sandy replied proudly, "Everything is needed… 5 T-shirts, 3 jeans, 2 shoes, 1 pair of trekking clothes, and full stock of snacks."

We all laughed.

By 7:30 the buses were ready. Students ran like mad to grab seats. Some wanted window, some wanted back seat, and some just wanted to sit next to their crush. There were four buses, one for each division.

The moment bus started, music also started, "Yeh laki kali aakhen" Bazigar songs blasted. It didn't take even five minutes for dance to begin.

Piddu was the first to stand in aisle, moving his shoulders, though his moves were completely off track with the Song.

Sandy joined him and within seconds half the bus was dancing. Teachers sitting in the front rows, gave up after two warnings.

In all this madness, Sandy slipped while trying some weird dance step and crashed straight onto a thin boy sitting in the aisle seat.

The poor fellow screamed like someone had stamped his tail. His voice was so loud that the driver almost hit the brakes, thinking some accident happened.

For a second we all got scared, the boy was holding his chest, breathing heavily, like he just saw Yamraj in front of him.

Piddu sarcastically shouted, "Bro, check fast his heart beats?"

Sandy kicked Piddu in anger.

Ashu bent dramatically and said, "Bro, move your fingers… okay, no fracture at least!"

Student screamed "I will do everything first ask this giant panda to stand and free me"

Sandy stood up, face red, trying to cover up, "Sorry bro… step got a little bit heavy. These songs have really tough moves!"

Piddu, who never misses a chance, shouted loudly, "May be it was little *heavy*!"

The whole bus roared with laughter. Some were holding stomach, some were banging seats. Even that thin boy, still rubbing his shoulder, couldn't stop laughing after two minutes. Teachers, who were trying hard to keep a straight face till now, finally gave up and laughed along with us.

From that moment, Sandy's fall officially became the "highlight dance step" of the night. Every time the next song started, someone would act like they're about to fall and shout, "Sorry bro!" and the whole bus would crack up again.

Journey continued with dance, antakshari, and random shouting. Somewhere past midnight, we crossed Gujarat border. The LLB gang, who were sitting in back, forced driver to stop for bio-break near a small shop which was next to a wine shop.

Within five minutes, the LLB gang along with few others pulled their stunt. The moment the bus stopped near that shop, two of them went for the "bio-break" while three others quietly walked towards the wine shop.

I thought they were just fooling around until I saw them suddenly lift one beer crate as if it was a bag of vegetables. They acted too cool, walking slowly at first, then in a flash they disappeared behind the bus.

From my window I could see the drama. Sandy inside the bus opened the back window, and from there Piddu started passing bottles like cricket fielding practice. Sam inside kept catching and sliding them under the last seat.

"This looks like smuggling scene from old Bollywood movie," Gayatri whispered, eyes wide.

By the time crate was empty, the shop owner realised something was wrong. He came running, shouting at the top of his lungs, "Oye, where are my bottles! Chor! Chor!"

Immediately, all the boys sat down innocently, faces straight, like they had just finished reciting Hanuman Chalisa. Sandy even yawned loudly to look extra casual.

The shopkeeper peeped inside the bus, but obviously couldn't find anything. The driver a scolded him, "What nonsense, don't disturb students." The man kept shouting for two minutes, then gave up as the bus started moving again.

The moment bus crossed danger zone of the shop, the last seat turned into bar counter. Bottles opened, cheers started, and suddenly the back of the bus was filled with smell of beer.

LLB boys were enjoying like kings. Piddu even raised his bottle and shouted, "To freedom!" Sandy added, "To Lonavalaaa!"

We all were half shocked, half laughing. Teachers sitting in front had no clue what was happening at the back.

Now the dance doubled, this time with beer. Songs got louder, moves got wilder from Sharukh style to Govinda style. Even teachers stopped interfering, maybe thinking it's better to ignore.

But beer also meant more bio-breaks. Around early morning, LLB gang again shouted, "Driver, stop! We can't hold anymore!" The bus halted in middle of dark jungle.

One teacher shouted "What are you guys doing that you need bio break again and again"

Sandy immediately replied "Motion sickness madam"

One by one, boys jumped out to relieve themselves. As usual, comedy followed Piddu.

Suddenly he shouted, "Areeeee… something stung me!" Everyone turned in shock.

Piddu ran towards bus, still peeing while running, screaming, " A bee stung on my penis!"

Girls screamed, boys laughed, teachers confused. Poor fellow splashed onto two students while running. Reaching near bus, he cried, "Give me water bottle, fast! I need to wash!"

Sandy was laughing so hard he fell on ground, holding his stomach. Girls were covering their eyes and shouting, "Disgusting!" but laughing at the same time.

It became the highlight of night. Even after bus started again, people kept teasing him:

"Red Panther turned in to Red Bee"

"Piddu, careful next time!"

"Bro, keep Dettol ready!"

"But who will apply"

The whole bus shook with laughter.

By the time dawn arrived, half the bus was asleep, half still singing. Everyone was tired but excited. Lonavala was waiting.

By next afternoon, after one full night of madness in the bus, we finally reached Lonavala. The moment bus stopped at the hotel, everyone looked half-dead. Hair messy, eyes red, voices cracked from nonstop shouting.

No one had energy left to do any more drama. We just dragged our bags inside, changed clothes, had quick lunch, and all of us collapsed like soldiers after war. I don't even remember when I fell asleep, it was a blackout nap.

When I woke up, the sun was already down. Evening lights were on, and excitement slowly started again. By 8 PM, a special dinner with dance was arranged. Everyone was fresh, dressed up, perfume in the air, energy back on full charge.

But before the party started, one incident happened.

I, Sandy, Piddu, and Sam were sitting near the swimming pool, lazily chatting, when we noticed Dinesh and Rishi sneaking away with two other boys. The way they walked careful, looking left and right, was enough to make us suspicious.

Sandy whispered, " Guys, see those guys, this looks fishy. Let's follow them."

So we quietly followed them, hiding behind bushes like RAW agents. After a few turns, we saw where they were standing, right behind the girls' wing. And not just standing, they were literally trying to peep inside one of the windows.

We froze.

"These idiots are trying to see the girls changing!" Piddu whispered, his eyes wide.

Sandy's blood boiled. He went straight to Dinesh and smacked him on the back of his head.

"You Bastards" he shouted.

Dinesh yelped in pain. The sound was so loud that the girls inside heard something. Within seconds, one of the curtains moved. It was Gayatri who opened it, trying to check what happened.

Our hearts stopped. All of us ducked behind the bush. Gayatri looked outside suspiciously, scanning the dark. She shouted, "Who's there?"

Nobody answered. She peeped out for a few seconds, saying softly, "Someone's definitely hiding..." and with doubt still on her face, she shut the curtain tight.

We all sat there holding our breath. Sandy glared at Dinesh, whispering angrily, "Go from here you bastards, don't try this ever again"

He kicked Dinesh. Reluctantly, they left.

I whispered, still confused, "Should we tell Sharma Sir about this?"

Sandy shook his head immediately, “Bro are you serious? Who will even believe us? They’ll think we were also part of the gang.”

He leaned closer and added, “Better we keep this as our secret only.

We headed back, hearts still racing but mouths refusing to stop laughing about how close the curtains had opened on us.

That little adventure became our secret.

It’s party time. Theme was black dress, and trust me, everyone looked like they had walked straight out of a Bollywood award show. Boys in black shirts, girls in black dresses, hair styled, jewellery shining, our simple school picnic had suddenly turned into cocktail night without the Alcohol.

Kabir also joined our group that evening. He had been hovering around ever since the ‘announcement’, but now he was fully planted with us.

The dinner hall was glowing with lights, music blasting. Students were dancing, laughing, enjoying.

Gayatri and I were sitting near the corner, chatting and laughing over the smallest things, who danced the worst, who was eating like it’s their last meal, and who was already planning the next dance move. Every time she laughed, she covered her mouth with her hand, and for some reason that made me laugh even more.

But Kabir had some other plans.

Every time I cracked a joke and made Gayatri laugh, Kabir would somehow slide in between, interrupting the conversation. Sometimes he asked unnecessary questions, sometimes he just stood there awkwardly, as if marking territory.

Piddu leaned in and whispered, “Why’s he acting like nightclub bouncer just because he wore black?”

I couldn’t help but laugh.

Dinner went on till past midnight, plates overloaded and dance steps getting worse with every new song.

At one point, Ashu and Piddu both were rolling on floor on their backs and trying to perform Nagin dance while Sam using his handkerchief trying to play snake pit.

Meanwhile, Sandy was forcing everyone to do the train dance. Half the crowd joined, half ran to save their legs. Even Sharma Sir, standing in the corner with his juice glass, had a tiny smile on his face, which itself was record-breaking.

By the time the last song ended, people were lying on chairs, shoes off, hair messy, but still shouting "One more! One more!"

That night, it felt like nobody wanted to sleep. For the first time, our whole batch, science, commerce, arts were dancing under one roof like a big crazy family.

Next morning everyone was woken up early by the teachers, though half the boys were still groaning like they hadn't slept in ten years. Somehow, after breakfast, all the buses rolled out for sightseeing.

Our bus went towards Tiger Point. The place was beautiful, fog rolling in, strong winds blowing, and that typical Lonavala vibe where even simple chai feels like heaven. The moment bus stopped, students jumped out.

Some went straight to click photos, some started shouting random songs, and the sporty ones began climbing the rocks nearby.

As expected, Piddu instantly became the centre of jokes. While everyone was adjusting cameras, one guy teased, "Piddu bro, want to take bio-break here also?"

The whole gang laughed, including the teachers. Even random strangers joined the laughter without knowing the story.

Piddu shook his head dramatically, "Yes, but somebody needs to help me in that."

Sandy added, "Next picnic we'll carry honey-bee repellent specially for you."

We almost fell rolling with laughter.

After a bit of trekking and photos, we all assembled at the lunch spot. Buses from other points also joined, so it was one big picnic mela again. Plates were served, students were sitting in groups, chatting and relaxing.

I was lying back on the grass with Sandy and Piddu when Kabir walked up. He looked unusually serious.

"Bro, I need to talk to you. Alone."

I frowned, "Now what?"

He nodded. "Yeah, just two minutes."

Curious, I got up and we walked a little away on a small trail. The breeze was strong, and the sound of people laughing behind us slowly faded.

Kabir finally spoke, his voice softer than usual.

"I wanted to tell you something… actually, I like Gayatri."

For a moment, I didn't know how to react. He continued quickly, "I want to tell her, but I need your help."

I stopped walking. "Help? Why me? You can directly tell her."

Kabir shook his head. "No, she listens to you. If you say something, she'll take it seriously. I'm afraid she won't even give me a chance otherwise."

I scratched my head, irritated. "But why should I? This doesn't make sense. If you like her, talk to her yourself. Don't drag me in between."

He looked desperate. "Please, Bro. Just once. Talk to her for me. At least I'll know what she feels. She'll give you an honest answer."

I stayed quiet. His eyes looked so intense that for a second I felt cornered.

After a pause, I sighed. "Fine… I'll try. But I don't guarantee anything."

Kabir's face lit up instantly. He hugged me, "Thanks, bro. I knew you'd understand."

As we walked back towards the crowd, Kabir looked relieved, almost smiling for the first time that day. But I wasn't smiling. Inside, it felt heavy.

Sandy called out, "What? Secret meeting with Kabir?" He winked.

I forced a smile, "Nothing like that. Just random talk."

I had a strange heaviness in my chest. On one side, it was just a favour for Kabir. But deep inside, I wasn't sure if I wanted to be the messenger at all.

That evening all of us headed towards the Sunset Point. The sky was glowing orange, cool wind blowing, and the whole place buzzing with students clicking photos like they had just discovered Instagram before time.

The LLB gang was of course in their own world, climbing rocks, making poses, forcing strangers to click their "candid" pictures. Sandy and Piddu were busy disturbing them, shouting, "Smile, Say Cheese or Paneer?" and running away before getting caught.

I quietly slipped away and sat on one big rock near the edge. Gayatri came and joined me.

Ashu came to us and said "Smile please" and click one candid picture of me and Gayatri sitting on the rock.

For a while, we both just sat there, watching the sun dip slowly. It was calm... maybe the only calm moment of the entire picnic.

I finally cleared my throat. "Umm... Gayatri, tell me something."

She turned, "What?"

I hesitated, then said slowly, "What do you think about all of us?"

She frowned, "All of us? What do you mean?"

"Generally, I'm asking," I replied, scratching my head. "We're not that studious, always doing masti... not really the serious type." I paused awkwardly.

She tilted her head, half-smiling. "Go on, Gopal. I know you're cooking something."

"Now Kabir also joined our group, he is talented, good in studies and sports… so I was just checking generally." I dragged my words, taking another long pause.

She rolled her eyes. "Gopal, I know you. You're very bad at these build-ups. Can you just come to the point?" Her voice was firm.

I raised my hand, "Okay, but promise me you won't get angry."

"I promise. Now say."

I took a deep breath. "Kabir came to me today. He confessed he likes you. He wanted me to tell you."

For a second, she was silent. She looked to the other side, but I caught that tiny smile.

I said softly, "So… is that an okay, not okay, or totally confused?"

She hit my shoulder lightly. After a pause she said, "Fine… no worries. I'll talk to him directly."

I just nodded. Inside me, a weird mix of relief and heaviness settled together.

After sunset we all went to our hotel.

That night was our last dinner party. The hall was decorated again, music blasting. Everyone was dressed up, full of energy.

During the party, Gayatri and Kabir were talking separately. After some time, she smiled and nodded, and then, we saw it. She hugged him.

The LLB gang, who were sitting nearby, noticed it too. For a moment, they all just exchanged surprised looks.

Sam said, "Guys, look there...finally… D-day came."

Sandy added, "Bro, come on, we all knew why Kabir was sticking around with us and Gayatri also liked his company, so honestly no surprise for me."

Piddu, scratching his head, whispered, "But at least someone should have warned us first… I would've carried a flower bouquet."

Sandy chuckled, "yaa, who would've known this was happening tonight?"

We all laughed.

After a while, Gayatri came over, her face glowing. She looked straight at me and said softly, "Thank you… for this."

I just nodded. She walked back, smiling and dancing with the girls.

The LLB gang looked at me with strange expressions, as if pieces of a puzzle had just clicked.

Piddu's comment came like a rocket, "Oh ho so you were the pandit who arranged this wedding!"

That set everyone laughing again.

And just like that, we merged back into the dinner party, plates full, music loud, laughter louder.

Later, Kabir also came, but his body language had changed. He wasn't the shy boy hanging around anymore. He looked confident, almost possessive, standing close to Gayatri all the time.

For the rest of us, the party continued, food, dance, laughter. But somewhere inside, I knew something had shifted.

What began as just another picnic of jokes and masti didn't end the same way. By that night, it was clear… one chapter of friendship was slipping away, while another story was taking shape.

– Navratri with Jungle Beats –

Present Day- 2025

All of a sudden, my phone buzzed.

I blinked. Memories in my head faded.

A message flashed on the screen,

"It's heavy traffic, will take more time to reach!"

"No worries, we are waiting for you guys" I replied.

I moved few things aside, and something small and colourful peeked out.

A rectangular piece of thick paper, edges curled, corners soft.

When I picked it up, I realised what it was.

A Garba pass.

The print had faded badly, but a few words were still visible,

"Garba '96 – Bhagra Club."

And just below that, half-erased numbers that probably said October 1996.

I smiled.

"Bhagra Club," I whispered to myself and laughed softly.

No one called it that anymore. It had been replaced by some fancy banquet hall years ago. But back then, in 1996, it was the place, loud music, bright lights and famous for its Garba nights.

I could almost hear it now, the beat of the dhol, the chorus of clapping.

The date on the pass blurred a little as I stared.

And before I knew it, I wasn't in my room anymore.

I was back there.

School days- 1996

Festive season had just begun. Navratri.

That one word was enough to change the mood of the entire city in fact of entire state.

Ahmedabad during Navratri was a different planet altogether. Streets were glowing with fairy lights, loudspeakers were testing dhol beats from every colony.

It was Friday afternoon, our usual adda under the neem tree was buzzing. The heat was still very strong, but the excitement of Navratri in the group was stronger.

Nidhi said "Guys,. what's the plan for the garba this weekend, have you decided for something for tomorrow's night?'

Sandy leaned back against the tree trunk, "Guys," he announced, "this year's garba at Bhagra Club is going to be epic. And guess what, your very own Sandy baba has managed some discount passes."

"Discount?" Sam smirked. "you bought passes or vegetables, like not your and not mine, let settle in between?"

Everyone laughed, but Sandy wasn't one to lose his spotlight. "Arre, joke all you want. But remember, Bhagra Club is the place. Proper lighting, live band, and girlssssss from all over the city."

Piddu already went in his imaginary world.

"Piddu come back" Nidhi giggled.

Sam's eyes widened. "Live band? Means they'll play actual dhol or that old uncle with a keyboard?"

Sandy rolled his eyes. "Bhai, you have no class. This is Bhagra Club. It's famous. People take loans just to buy passes."

Everyone burst out laughing.

Decision was made. Saturday night. Bhagra Club. Meeting point: Piddu's house. His house was closest, and more importantly, his father's scooter was available. That meant transport tension solved. Nidhi decided to come with Gayatri.

We all were very excited and planning about Saturday night. But as usual, Gayatri wasn't there. These days, it had become routine. Since she started dating Kabir, her appearances during lunch were like comet sightings, rare and unpredictable.

Sam suddenly sat up. "By the way, where is madam Gayatri these days? Always missing."

Sandy smirked knowingly. "Where else? With Kabir. She must be having her own private adda."

The laughter came, but not from me. I kept quiet.

Over the past few months, things had changed quietly. Gayatri was still around, technically. But the closeness we once had, those random jokes, inside nicknames, late evening talks, all of it had slowly faded away.

It started slowly. First, Kabir began joining us for lunch sometimes. He wasn't rude, just... stiff. Like a guest who didn't really want to be there but came anyway because his girlfriend insisted. He'd sit, smile politely, and the moment our conversation turned funny or personal, his smile would tighten like a screw.

Later, Gayatri's visits became fewer. First, she stopped coming to lunch. Then, she started taking a different bus home, a longer route, she claimed. "Kabir also takes that route," she had explained once, avoiding my eyes.

We understood. But it still stung a little.

That night, my phone rang. It was Gayatri. For a moment, I just stared at the ringing phone, surprised.

"Hello?" I said, trying to sound casual.

"Hey," her voice came, soft, hurried. "I've arranged your pass also for tomorrow. Bhagra Club. Nidhi and I will come there directly."

I blinked. "Oh, okay. But Sandy is arranging it"

"Do you have any problem if i have arranged it for you" She said with some anger

"No.. I mean...Thanks."

"Cool. See you then."

And that was it. She hung up.

I sat there, staring at the phone. It wasn't a long call. Barely thirty seconds. But my heart felt heavier and lighter at the same time.

Heavier, because the distance was obvious now. Lighter, because at least she remembered me.

Saturday evening arrived with the kind of buzz that only festivals bring. The whole city felt alive, music playing from every corner.

By six, I was already on the bus to Piddu's house. The bus was packed, of course half the city was probably heading to garba. Somehow, I managed to get down near Piddu's lane, clutching my kurta like it was a precious artefact.

Piddu's house was easy to spot. He lived in one of those old Gujarati societies, small bungalow-type houses, lined neatly next to each other like family members at a wedding photo. There were maybe twenty, twenty-five houses in total, all standing proudly for the last fifteen, twenty years.

The moment you entered, you could feel that old Ahmedabad charm. The main door of every house was open, that's how it always is in these societies. My mom once said, in old Gujarati homes, doors are never shut. It's a tradition, a sign that anyone is welcome, neighbour, guest, anyone.

You could hear the sounds of evening life, steel plates clinking from kitchens, the smell of fresh thepla in the air. From one house came the sweet sound of aarti, the bell ringing in rhythm. Somewhere, a radio played an old Garba song.

People were sitting outside their homes, on charpais or plastic chairs, chatting about everything from cricket scores to someone's daughter's rishta. The moment they saw me entering, a few aunties paused their conversation mid-sentence. Their eyes followed me like radars, not out of suspicion, just pure curiosity. In such societies, nobody needs CCTV cameras; the aunties are more efficient and available 24x7.

One aunty even asked, "Beta, tame kona ghar jao cho?" (Son, whose house are you visiting?) I smiled and said, "Piddu na. Ummm Pradeep na" She nodded knowingly, as if she already had a full family history of Piddu stored in her mental database.

It took barely three or four minutes to walk from the main gate to his house, but in that short time, I had been scanned, analysed, and approved by at least six aunties, two uncles, and one dog sitting at the corner.

That's how you know you've entered an old Gujarati mohalla, every step feels like you're walking through someone's extended family.

Inside, Piddu was wiping his father's Bajaj scooter like it was a Ferrari. His hair was soaked in sweat, and his shirt had more polish stains than a mechanic's apron.

"Bro, you are polishing or painting it?" I laughed.

"Arre, boss, presentation matters! What if girls see us arrive? Scooter should shine like hero entry," he said proudly, rubbing one last patch

Before I could reply, Sandy arrived, swinging his brother's bike keys like a Tollywood Hero.

"Gentlemen," he said, posing dramatically, "your captain has arrived. Bhagra Club, prepare yourself for history."

Sam followed right behind him, "I hope this historical place will have snacks. I'm starving."

"Snacks?" Piddu's face lit up. "Let's go to Ramesh Bhai's stall before we leave. His pani puri is calling me."

Sandy groaned. "Pani puri before garba? Bhai, you'll end up dancing near the toilet."

"Better toilet than empty stomach," Piddu shot back.

Ten minutes later, the entire gang was standing around Ramesh Bhai's cart. The air was filled with the smell of spicy pani puris.

Piddu, as usual, went first. "Bhai, spicy banana. Extra spicy!"

Ramesh Bhai raised an eyebrow. "Are you sure? Last time you cried."

"That was acting," Piddu said proudly.

Four- Five puris later, his eyes were red, nose running, and he was gasping like a fish.

Sandy patted his back. "Next time, just swallow mirchi directly, faster result."

Everyone burst out laughing as Piddu tried to speak between hiccups. "Bhai... it's... not spicy... it's... emotional pani puri."

Sam joined in. "It's not a pani puri, it's an emotional atyachar!"

We followed it up with samosa chaat, dahi puri, and a few unnecessary jokes about digestion. The crowd was building up around the stall, kids, couples, aunties bargaining for an extra puri like their life depended on it.

Finally, we checked the time. Forty-five minutes left for garba to start. Perfect.

Back at Piddu's house, the final vehicle discussion began.

"So," Sandy said, "I'll take my brother's bike. Sam, you're behind me."

Piddu nodded. "And you, my dear friend," he pointed at me, "will have the honour of sitting behind Bajaj super 1992 model. Strong, reliable, slightly emotional."

I laughed. "Fine. But make sure it runs. I don't want to push it halfway."

"Don't worry," he said proudly, "I poured one full mug of petrol this morning."

Sandy looked horrified. "A *mug*? What's that, new metric unit?"

"Arre, don't tease him," Sam said. "At least he has petrol. Sandy's bike runs on confidence."

"Not Sandy's bike, his brother's borrowed bike" Piddu winked

Everyone started laughing again. The air was full of madness, where jokes have no logic but laughter feels endless.

Just then, Piddu's father stepped out, holding his evening tea. "Where guys?"

"Garba, Papa. Bhagra Club," Piddu said.

His father nodded. "Good.. Good. Which route you guys are taking Pradeep, its bit far?"

"Shortcut through the small jungle patch. Saves one hour."

His father paused, sipping his tea slowly. "Hmm… okay. Just be careful. That area used to be graveyard. You might find stones on the road. But it's only 3–4 kilometres, nothing to worry."

For a moment, we all froze.

Graveyard.

Even the word sent a shiver through the group.

Sandy looked at me, eyes wide. "Did he just say *graveyard*?"

Piddu's father walked back inside casually, as if he'd said, "Watch out for a speed bump."

I whispered, "Graveyard? Bro, are you sure about this route?"

Piddu tried to laugh it off. "Arre, come on, don't overthink. It's Navratri, ghosts are on holiday."

Sam added, "Yeah, they must be busy dancing somewhere else."

Sandy puffed his chest. "Koi gal nahi, are we less than ghosts? Ask principal madam."

We burst out laughing again, trying to shake off the chill. But somewhere deep down, everyone was just a little uneasy.

Still, excitement won. We loaded our stuff and stood ready, four friends in kurta pyjamas, one scooter, one bike, and unlimited stupidity.

As we started the engines, Sandy shouted, "Let's go make Bhagra Club proud!"

And with that, our mini convoy rolled into the night, unaware that the shortcut we'd just chosen would give us a story we'd be telling for years.

We hit the road with full excitement, two vehicles, four idiots, and one overconfident shortcut plan.

Sandy led the way on his brother's bike, and Piddu followed behind on the mighty Bajaj scooter. The road started out smooth, with the occasional cow standing like a philosopher in the middle of the lane.

Music was playing from someone's house nearby, garba beats floating through the air, "Tara Vina Shyam Mane Ekalu Lage Re…"

For a moment, it felt festive, peaceful.

But soon, the houses disappeared. The lights faded. The road narrowed into a dusty trail.

"This must be the jungle patch your papa mentioned," I said.

Piddu nodded, but his shoulders stiffened. "Yeah, but it's only 3–4 kilometres, na?. We'll be out soon."

The darkness was thick now. The only light came from the scooter's dim yellow headlamp, which flickered like it was scared as well. Crickets chirped somewhere in the background, and once in a while, a dry leaf crackled under the tyres, making our hearts jump unnecessarily.

Out of nowhere, Piddu started chanting under his breath. "Om namah shivaya… Om namah shivaya…"

Sandy looked back, grinning. "Arre, what's this? Feeling spiritual?"

"Safety protocol, bro," said Piddu seriously. "In case ghosts are watching, they should know we have God's backing."

We all laughed, though a little nervously.

Ten minutes into the ride, everything was fine, until suddenly, the scooter sputtered and came to a stop.

Piddu hit the brakes. "What happened?" I asked.

He didn't reply. He just sat there, gripping the handle tightly.

"Why did you stop?" Sandy called out from ahead.

No answer.

Then, slowly, Piddu turned towards me. His face looked tense, eyes wide. "Bro… it's an emergency."

"What emergency?"

He whispered, "Pani puri emergency."

"What!?"

"Bhai, that spicy one from Ramesh Bhai… it's doing *garba* inside my stomach. I can't hold it anymore."

Sandy nearly fell off his bike laughing. "Are you serious? *Here?* In the middle of a jungle?"

"I don't have a choice!" Piddu said, already jumping off the scooter. "Either I go now, or it'll come by itself!"

We were speechless.

"Someone give water!" Piddu shouted, half bent, clutching his stomach.

"Water?" Sam started checking his bag in panic. "Wait, wait… I've got chips, one banana, and" he pulled out a half packet of *Parle G*, "biscuit helps?"

"Idiot!" Piddu groaned. "I need *water*, not carbs!"

" If it helps, we'll pee together. Team spirit!"" Sam grinned.

Sandy was already laughing. "Bhai, even ghosts won't have mercy if you do your business without water."

We all looked around helplessly. Empty road. No tap, no bottle, not even a puddle. Only dust and darkness.

Piddu looked like a man on the edge. "Forget it! I'll manage!"

"Manage how?" Sam asked, half-concerned, half-curious.

That's when Piddu's eyes landed on something under the scooter seat, an old, crumpled copy of *Gujarat Samachar*. Probably his father's from last week.

His face lit up like he'd found gold. "Jai ho Gujarat Samachar!" he declared dramatically, snatched it, and ran behind a tree.

Sandy shouted after him, "Arre, don't read the headlines now! Do your work first!"

We all burst out laughing.

Piddu rushed towards the nearest tree and began his urgent offloading.

Behind the tree, we could still hear him muttering, "Om Namah Shivaya… Om Namah Shivaya…" like he was performing a purification ritual instead of… well, you know.

Sam folded his arms, dead serious. "Bhai, I think this is the first time Gujarat Samachar will actually serve the public."

That finished us. We laughed so hard that even the ghosts, if there were any, must've thought *these guys are hopeless.*

That's when we heard it, a low coughing sound from somewhere inside the bushes.

All laughter stopped.

It wasn't the wind. It was real. A harsh, dry *kha…kha…* sound.

Sandy's eyes widened. "Did you hear that?"

"Yes!" I whispered. "Piddu! Jaldi kar!"

No reply.

"Bhai, I think someone's there," Sam whispered, clutching my arm.

"Someone or something?" Sandy muttered dramatically.

"Shut up!" I hissed. My voice came out lower than I expected. "Piddu, come fast!"

We all held our breath, eyes fixed on the dark patch of trees. Every second felt longer than an exam minute.

Another *cough*, this time, closer.

And then, out of the darkness, Piddu came running, pants half up, one hand clutching the Gujarat Samachar. His face was pale, eyes wide as if he'd seen the devil.

"Chalo! Chalo! Start the scooter!" he shouted.

Sandy had already started his bike and taken off. I jumped onto the scooter, yelling,

"God, Piddu! Tell me you used the newspaper, please! I can fight ghosts, but not this smell!"

"Shut up" Piddu tried to kick-start it.

Nothing.

He tried again. Kick after kick, still nothing.

"Arre, check ignition!" Sam yelled.

Piddu looked down. The ignition was off.

He turned it on. The scooter roared to life.

"Go!" I shouted.

And Piddu went.

Full throttle. Like a man possessed.

The road was full of potholes, uneven like a bad haircut. The scooter jumped, rattled, and at one point, I swear we caught air.

"Piddu, wait, slow down!" I shouted.

He didn't listen. His only mission: escape the ghosts.

The scooter was dancing like a ship in a storm. I was holding on for life.

"Stop! Stop!" I kept yelling.

He didn't.

Finally, after what felt like an eternity, the bright lights of Bhagra Club appeared in the distance. Music, people, the smell of popcorn, civilization!

Only then did he hit the brakes. The scooter screeched to a stop right outside the gate.

Piddu jumped off, threw the scooter stand down, and ran straight to the washroom without saying a word.

I was still sitting there, panting. My legs felt weirdly numb.

Sandy and Sam parked behind us, laughing so hard they could barely stand. "What a ride!"

Sandy said. "Bhai, you looked like you were hanging from a helicopter!"

I stood up and turned around to show the back of the scooter.

"Do you know why I was shouting 'stop'?" I said.

They looked.

The scooter's back seat cushion was *missing*. It had fallen off somewhere in the jungle.

Only the metal frame was left, full of sharp edges.

"For the last fifteen minutes," I said, "I was standing on that thing. My legs were vibrating like a generator."

Everyone exploded into laughter. Even a few random people at the gate turned to look.

"Bhai, you're legend!" said Sandy between laughs. "Next time we'll bring your seat separately!"

I just shook my head, trying not to laugh too much. The fear, the chaos, the laughter, it was all mixed up now.

Somewhere behind us, music from the club was getting louder. Garba night had begun.

The club entrance looked like a film set, colourful banners, flashing lights, security guards pretending to check passes but mostly checking people's outfits. Inside, it was chaos in the best way. Dhol beats vibrated in the air, girls twirled in their bright chaniya cholis, and boys tried to look like they actually knew how to dance.

We stood for a moment, soaking it all in. Navratri nights like this had their own magic, nine days when the whole city forgot stress, heartbreak, and electricity bills.

And then, through the crowd, I saw her.

Gayatri.

She was standing near the gate with Nidhi, laughing at something.

Sandy spotted her too. "Arre dekho, madam finally arrived!"

When she saw us, her face lit up in surprise. "Hey! You guys actually came!"

Sandy replied, "Came? We almost *died* to come. Ask this fellow." He pointed at me.

Gayatri frowned, confused. "What happened?"

And that's when Sandy started the storytelling marathon. "Madam, your friend Piddu decided to challenge ghosts tonight. Then he fought with his stomach, lost, and performed a dance behind a tree with *Gujarat Samachar* as his partner!"

Nidhi burst out laughing so loud people around turned to look. "You're kidding!"

I shook my head. "No, unfortunately not. I was witness. Still suffering."

Even Gayatri laughed, covering her mouth. "You guys are crazy."

For a moment, it felt normal again, like we were back to our old gang days. Same laughter, same teasing. The small wall between us almost disappeared.

But then came the sound I wasn't expecting.

"Hey, there you are," said a voice behind her.

Kabir.

He walked up, dressed sharply in a navy blue kurta, looking every bit the confident guy he always tried to be. His eyes flicked over me and then to the group. His smile was polite, but there was something else behind it, that silent measuring look.

"Hi, everyone," he said.

"Hi," we replied, almost in chorus.

He looked around. "Garba here isn't that great this year. I've got passes for another club, much better music, proper crowd. I can get two extra entries for Gayatri and Nidhi."

There it was.

A simple statement, but it hit deeper than we expected.

Sandy blinked. "Oh… only two passes?"

Kabir nodded. "Yeah, limited entries. I tried my best."

Gayatri looked unsure. She turned to us. "Umm… maybe we can join you guys later?"

Sandy tried to smile. "Yeah, sure. Go ahead. We'll manage here."

I didn't say anything. Just nodded.

Kabir placed his hand lightly on her shoulder, and within minutes, they were gone into the crowd. The music suddenly felt louder, but emptier.

Nidhi turned once before leaving and gave a small wave.

And just like that, half the gang was gone.

For a while, we stood there quietly, trying to pretend it didn't matter. Sam broke the silence first. "So… shall we dance?"

"Of course," Sandy said.

We all laughed, though half-heartedly. We went inside the club and straight away joined the circle, pretending to enjoy. The lights spun around, dhols beat faster, but the rhythm inside us was missing. It wasn't the same without everyone together.

After the half round, Sandy stopped. "Bhai, this doesn't feel fun."

"Yeah," Sam said. "Let's go. We'll grab chai outside."

We stepped out quietly. The crowd behind us cheered louder, as if mocking our mood.

Outside, sitting on the scooter again, I watched the people going in, couples, friends, strangers, all lost in the festive chaos. I couldn't help but smile a little.

Piddu came out from the washroom at last, wiping his face. "Bhai, what did I miss?"

Sandy grinned weakly. "Everything."

And as the music from Bhagra Club echoed behind us, we rode away slowly, four friends on two vehicles, heading into the night that suddenly didn't feel so festive anymore.

We stopped at a small tea stall near the highway, the kind that stays open till late during Navratri season. Dim bulb, wooden benches, and a sleepy owner making tea like he was performing a religious ritual.

Sandy ordered four chais. We sat there silently, watching the steam rise.

Sandy finally broke the silence. "You know what, bhai, Kabir is always with that smug look, like he's the CEO of some company."

Sam chuckled. "CEO! Good one."

Piddu added, "And Gayatri just follows him. She used to lead our group once. Remember? She was the one shouting at us to reach on time for events."

"Yeah," I said quietly. "People change."

"Remember last year's Navratri?" Sam said suddenly. "Gayatri was the one teaching us garba steps. You almost twisted your leg."

Sandy smiled faintly. "Yeah. She said I danced like a malfunctioning robot."

Everyone laughed softly. It was strange, how laughter could sit right next to sadness without feeling out of place.

"Maybe it's just a phase," I said after a while. "Relationships change people. Once the newness goes, things will settle."

Sandy snorted. "Or maybe they won't. Some people never come back, bhai. They just become stories you tell at chai stalls."

That hit harder than he probably intended.

The tea arrived, and for a few minutes, none of us spoke. Just the sound of spoons clinking and traffic in the distance.

Then Sandy looked up. "You know, even if she doesn't come around, it's fine. We'll still have each other. LLB gang zindabad."

Piddu raised his cup. "LLB gang zindabad!"

We all clinked our tiny glasses like it was a toast to lost times.

When I reached home later that night, the house was quiet. My parents were asleep. I changed clothes and lay down, staring at the ceiling fan turning slowly above. My legs still hurt from standing on that metal scooter seat, but my heart hurt more.

I kept thinking about that moment at the club, the way Gayatri smiled briefly before walking away with Kabir. It didn't hurt as much as I expected. Maybe because somewhere, I already knew this is how life works.

People come close, they laugh, they share stories, they feel like family, and then one day, the distance starts. Not with a fight or a reason, just quietly.

It starts with fewer calls, shorter messages, different plans, new people. Slowly, what was once everyday becomes "once in a while." And before you even realise, the circle changes.

That's just how it goes, I guess, stranger, friend, bonding, distance, and then stranger again.

I smiled to myself. It wasn't sadness anymore. Just a kind of peace, knowing that some people are meant to walk with you only for a few chapters, not the whole book.

And maybe that's fine.

Because even if they leave, they still leave something behind, a memory, a laugh, a story that still makes you smile when you think about it on quiet nights.

The strain that broke the 'Bond'

Present Day- 2025

The door of my room opened.

My wife peeked in.

"How much more time will you take, Gopal? They may reach any time now," she said.

I blinked, coming back to the present.

"I got a message," I replied, glancing at my phone on the bed. "They're stuck in traffic. It'll take a little more time."

"Okay, but please come out fast,"

She smiled faintly, closed the door, and left.

The room fell silent again.

Digging a little deeper into the box, my hand touched something soft, not paper or plastic.

I pulled it out carefully, and there it was, my **old white T-shirt.**

The fabric had turned a little yellow with age, but the print on the front was still readable:

"Karnavati Vidyalaya, Shahibaug."

I turned it around.

On the back, in bold blue letters, it said:

"Sardar House."

And right below that, my name,

"Gopal."

I smiled.

The shirt still carried a faint stain near the collar. The same tear from *that fall* during the volleyball final match.

I ran my fingers over it and laughed softly.

I held it against myself, trying to picture how it once fit me.

God.

I couldn't believe I'd ever been that thin.

That T-shirt wouldn't even make it past my head now.

I shook my head, still smiling.

I looked at the T-shirt again, the faded print, the uneven stitches.

Memories flashed in my mind, one slip, one tumble, and there I was, shoulder torn, elbow bruised, with Gayatri shouting from the other side.

School days- 1996

Our pre-board exams were around the corner. We had only sports week in between and then our final struggle would start. Day by day atmosphere in the class grew tense.

The day began with dull periods first Accountancy, where Sharma Sir revised a few chapters on inventory valuation, period followed by Geography, and then Hindi.

Now it's the last period before the lunch time and it was with Bhatia Madam.

"Guys I am too hungry now... I desperately need Samosas... I quick go and get some" Sandy said.

"Are you crazy, its Bhatia Madam's class. Don't even try this" I said.

Meanwhile Bhatia madam entered the classroom, her face carrying the same expression as always, like she had a fight over breakfast at home in the morning.

She placed her handbag on the desk with the thud of a judge announcing a death sentence and said in her usual flat voice,

"Today… we will do the revision."

The entire class groaned silently. Revision meant random questions fired like bullets, and you could never predict whose head they'd hit.

Bhatia madam scanned the room like a CCTV camera.

"You… Ravi… define utility."

Ravi stood up and said in a single breath "Utility is the satisfaction, happiness, or benefit that a consumer gets from consuming a good or service. This concept is central to understanding consumer behaviour, market demand, and pricing"

"Is there any chapter on Utility in Economics" Piddu whispered

We both smiled while looking down.

"That's my boy, class clap for him."

Entire class applauded.

"You, Shalini, what is opportunity cost?"

Shalini, with full confidence, said, "opportunity cost is the value of the next-best alternative that must be forgone when a choice is made. It is a fundamental principle that arises because resources—such as money, time, and labour—are scarce, meaning there are not enough resources to satisfy all human wants. This necessitates making trade-offs, and opportunity cost represents the potential benefits lost by not pursuing the best alternative.

"This too is there" Piddu whispered again

Entire class applauded without waiting Madam to say that.

"Guys i am too much hungry do you have anything to eat, or else I can't survive for a minute now" Sandy whispered.

This time his whispered was loud enough to reach Bhatia madam's ears.

"Oh... now it's time to hear something intellectual.... Sandeep... explain the Law of Marginal Utility."

"Marginal Utility again" Sandy whispered.

The entire class looked at Sandy. We knew this was not going to end well.

Sandy stood... looking here and there. Then preparing himself to reply.

"Sandy don't... pls don't bluff..." I thought, staring at him like a bomb about to explode.

I knew that sandy had a dangerous habit: whenever he didn't know something, he invented his own version with full confidence, and he was never afraid to say anything.

Sandy cleared his throat, and began.

"Madam, allow me to explain the Law of Marginal Utility with an example rather than plain English..."

"Oh wow, with example ... very nice. Go on, go on. Class, pay attention, this will clear all your concepts." Madam said, dripping with sarcasm.

Class chuckled.

"When one eats too many samosas, at first the happiness is high, but slowly, happiness goes down. Because chutney gets over. And finally... stomach pain."

The class erupted.

Madam raised her eyebrows, "What is this Samosa and chutney theory, Sandeep?"

But Sandy wasn't done. Once his engine started, no one could stop him.

"Madam, wait... I am coming to marginal utility," Sandy replied proudly.

"Ohh, from samosa to marginal utility. What a journey." Madam's sarcasm continued, making the class roar.

"Yes Madam, Marginal utility also applies to love. First day of dating, very high happiness. By third month, you are bored, by sixth month, finished."

The girls in the class started laughing louder than the boys.

Madam tried to control him.

"Enough, Sandeep. Stick to the law."

But Sandy raised his hand like a philosopher giving gyaan.

"Madam, one second. I will also connect this to the Law of Demand and Supply. Because if samosa supply goes down, my demand goes up. And if samosa supply goes up, my demand still goes up."

Now the whole class was howling. Even I had tears in my eyes from laughing.

But Sandy's masterpiece was yet to come.

"Also, madam, one should not forget the Law of Gravity. Because after eating too many samosas, one has to lie down. Gravity pulls us to bed. That is also marginal utility."

The class went wild. Benches were shaking.

Madam, who was always famous for her serious face, finally broke. She burst into laughter. A real laugh, loud and open, like we had never seen before. For the first time, Bhatia Madam was not just a teacher, but one of us.

Sandy looked proud. He had achieved something no economist could do—he made Bhatia Madam laugh.

She shook her head and said,

"Sandeep, you are hopeless... sit down before I fail you in the exam."

The class was still shaking with laughter, a few students even kept clapping as if Sandy had just given a stage performance.

"Thank you madam" Sandy sat down, grinning, whispering to me,

"Samosa saved me today."

The rest of the period passed in that rare cheerful mood. For once, revision felt like entertainment. Nobody remembered the question, but everybody remembered Sandy's Samosa and chutney theory of economics.

The bell rang for lunch break.

For us, lunch break had only one address, the big palm tree near the boundary wall. Our permanent adda. Dusty ground, uneven roots, but more comfortable than any sofa in the world.

Sandy dropped down on the grass like a wrestler after a match. "Finally Samosas, my love. you are here "

Piddu opened his tiffin and groaned, "Again karela sabzi! I think my parents fought last night... Mom cooked this to punish Dad, and I became the collateral damage."

Nidhi pulled out her paratha roll, " Smell this, Piddu."

We all booed her.

The adda was always the same: half gossip, half food exchange, and full-time nonsense. Someone always trying to steal someone else's tiffin, Sandy explaining why samosas should be part of the syllabus.

I looked around. Gayatri wasn't there.

Earlier, she was always the first to sit under this palm tree, arguing with Sandy, scolding Piddu, teasing me. Now it was different. She'd come late, or sometimes not at all.

Sandy noticed my silence and nudged me. "Don't worry, Gopal. She's now president of Kabir's gang."

Piddu added with a grin, "Next week she'll start wearing black goggles in class like a gang member. Guarantee."

Nidhi smirked, "Or maybe Kabir will carry her books like a bodyguard."

Everyone laughed.

We were still laughing at "Kabir will carry her books" joke when suddenly the laughter froze.

Gayatri was walking towards us. Fast. Almost running. And right behind her, Kabir.

Her face was red, her eyes sharp. She looked like someone who had marched straight out of a Bollywood climax scene. Even the breeze around the palm tree seemed to pause.

She didn't even glance at Sandy, Piddu, or Nidhi. She came straight to me.

"Gopal… I want some answers."

Kabir reached her side, trying to calm her down.

"Gayatri, relax… not here….."

"Don't stop me, Kabir!" she snapped, brushing his hand off.

I didn't say anything. My brain was searching for clues. What had happened? Why was she looking at me like I had committed murder?

The adda, which was usually full of noise, turned into a graveyard. Sandy's mouth stayed open, but no words came out. Even Piddu stopped chewing mid-bite.

I could feel everyone around slowing down too. Students walking past us had reduced their speed, clearly eavesdropping. Some even pretended to tie their shoelaces right there, just to not miss the drama.

Gayatri's eyes were fixed on me, burning, like she wanted to see straight inside my head.

I stayed silent.

"Gopal," she repeated, her voice sharper this time, "I said I want some answers."

I still stayed silent.

"During the picnic… there were boys who tried to peep inside the girls' window."

The world stopped.

For a second, nobody moved. Even Sandy, who always had some nonsense ready. My heartbeat jumped. That incident… it was supposed to be buried forever. No one outside our gang even knew.

"How… how does she know?" I thought, my throat drying.

She stepped closer, her voice shaking but sharp.

"Tell me the truth, Gopal, there were boys who tried to peep inside the girls' window?"

I looked straight into her eyes. My silence was heavy, louder than any words.

Gayatri's face turned harder.

"Answer me!"

"Yes," I said finally, my voice firm, without hesitation.

Gasps around us. Sandy's head snapped towards me. Piddu muttered something under his breath. Nidhi's eyes widened.

But Gayatri wasn't done. She moved a little closer and said.

"You were also there?"

That question hit me like a bullet straight to the chest.

I stood frozen, my mind blank. The truth was twisted, the situation poisoned. My lips struggled.

"Yes… but….."

The word didn't even leave my mouth completely before it happened.

Smack.

Her hand landed on my face, sharp, sudden, echoing louder than the bell.

Sandy jumped up, "Gayatri, listen......."

I raised my hand quickly.

"Don't. Let her speak."

Gayatri's eyes were wet now, but her voice roared.

"How could you, Gopal? You knew I was in that room, and still you tried to do that? How could you stoop so low?"

Sandy clenched his fists, "This is rubbish...."

"Quiet!" she snapped. Her voice cracked but didn't soften.

"I don't trust Sandy, I don't trust Piddu. But you..." She looked at me again, her eyes flooding.

"You were my best friend. And you did this to me. I feel ashamed."

Her tears rolled down, one after another, faster than I had ever seen.

I kept looking into her eyes, but words refused to come.

That single word '*were*' hit harder than the slap.

Sandy couldn't hold back anymore. He sprang to his feet.

"Gayatri, mind your language! You don't even know the truth!"

She turned sharply, eyes blazing.

"I don't need your truth, Sandy. I heard enough."

Piddu finally spoke, his voice shaking with anger.

"This is nonsense! You are twisting our character! Someone's poisoned your mind!"

"Shut up!" she shouted, her voice echoing.

"One yes from Gopal was enough. That's all I need to hear."

I raised my hand again, stopping both Sandy and Piddu.

"Don't say anything. Let her finish."

Gayatri's lips trembled. She looked at me one last time.

"You broke something that can't be fixed, Gopal. You broke the trust and the friendship forever."

Her words cut deeper than the slap.

She turned away quickly, wiping her eyes.

Kabir stayed a step behind, his face cold.

Before leaving, he looked at us and said in a low, sharp tone,

"Stay away from her, guys."

And just like that, they were gone.

For a long moment, none of us spoke. We just sat there under the palm tree.

The adda that was always full of laughter suddenly felt like a courtroom after the judge had declared everyone guilty.

Sandy broke the silence first, slamming his palm on the ground.

"Why didn't you let me speak, Gopal? I would have cleared everything right there!"

Piddu shook his head violently.

"Exactly! She was talking rubbish, twisting our character, and you just stood like a statue. We should have explained, we should have fought back."

I didn't look at them. I was still staring at the spot where Gayatri had stood, her eyes wet, her words sharper than glass.

Finally, I spoke softly.

"If she needed an explanation to trust us, then maybe the friendship was already broken or maybe it was never friendship at all."

Sandy leaned closer, his voice rising.

"Don't talk like that! She's our friend, bro. She's been tricked, can't you see? This is Kabir and Dinesh's handiwork. They poisoned her."

Piddu nodded furiously.

"They've been waiting since that night. This is their revenge. And Gayatri… she just fell for it. Blindly."

I sighed, my hand rubbing my cheek where her slap still burned.

"She didn't fall blindly, Piddu. She believed them because she wanted to. That's the truth."

Silence again. Heavy, choking silence.

For once, even Sandy had no answer. He just stared at the ground, fists clenched.

But the only voice stuck in my head was hers.

"You WERE my best friend."

Were. Past tense. That word alone felt heavier than everything else.

I closed my eyes, and for the first time, our adda under the palm tree didn't feel like home. It felt like a battlefield we had already lost.

Maybe that's how bonds break, not with a fight, not with a grand goodbye, but with one sentence and one slap.

I thought of all those afternoons when Gayatri sat here with us, scolding Sandy for stealing food, laughing at Piddu's hopeless jokes, teasing me till I lost my patience. All those memories now stood in front of me like strangers.

And the worst part? She didn't even wait to hear me out.

That was enough for me to know. The chapter of our friendship wasn't just hurt. It was ended.

Sports Day - 'The fall'

Things had changed between the LLB gang and Gayatri after that day.

She had stopped talking to us completely, behaving as if we didn't even exist.

Sports Day was announced around this time, the last big event of the year before exam fever would officially hijack our lives.

Earlier, we used to make so many plans for every event like what to do, how to do, even silly stunts to pull off. But now, all of that excitement had faded. The mood had changed in the LLB gang.

Sports Day was coming. The announcements were done, teams were being formed, and houses were getting ready to fight like it was the Olympics, not just a sweaty school ground.

Our school had four houses—Raman House, Tagore House, Ashoka House, and our mighty Sardar House. And as luck (or maybe managed by Sandy) would have it, the entire LLB gang was in Sardar House. That meant, win or lose, we were stuck together.

We were all participating some or other game.

Everyone in the school was going crazy with excitement. Posters were made, slogans prepared, and house leaders were barking orders like politicians before elections.

Sandy, of course, went straight for kabaddi. With his size, no one even argued. Sam and I landed in volleyball. And Piddu… well, he was strangely secretive about his event.

The air was thick with competition. Every house wanted to crush the other, every student wanted a medal.

The stage was ready.

Here comes the Sports day.

On the morning of Sports Day, the school ground looked like a mela. Flags tied to bamboo poles, white chalk lines freshly drawn, and kids running around in white canvas shoes that were white only till the first race began.

But one question haunted us: Where is Piddu?

We searched everywhere, the class room, our usual adda, even the shady tree near the cycle stand where he usually hid. No sign.

"Don't tell me he bunked Sports Day also," Sam said, panting.

Sandy shook his head, "Impossible. He must be cooking some scheme."

There he was, standing in the badminton court, holding a racket upside down, practicing like a serious pro.

"What is this? Seriously!" I shouted, running towards him. "Piddu, you don't even know the difference between badminton and lawn tennis. Since when are you a player?"

Piddu gave his trademark grin. "Bro, relax. This is called hidden talent."

Sandy raised his eyebrows. "Hidden talent? Or hidden intention?

"And that too in mixed doubles! By the way, who's your partner?" I asked, pretending to be curious.

"Aparna," Piddu replied, blushing like he'd just proposed.

The three of us froze.

"Aparna that Girls from XII-D Arts that?" Sandy asked

"Yes, yes, same Aparna," Piddu replied proudly.

Sandy almost choked on his own laughter. "Since when, Piddu?"

Piddu winked. "Ekdum latest hai."

"Just remember, badminton is played with a shuttle, not a tennis ball," Sandy teased, shaking his head.

That was enough. We burst out laughing.

Piddu, without missing a beat, shot back, "Chal..chal, don't try teaching father how to make babies!"

Aparna came forward, gave Piddu a polite handshake. But Piddu? He kept shaking her hand like his hand had been magnet-stuck to hers.

The referee blew the whistle and the match began.

Aparna looked serious. Proper stance, eyes on the shuttle, like a proper Olympics player. And Piddu? His stance looked less like a player and more like a bodyguard, hovering dangerously close to her, few inches far from her.

Every time Aparna moved to hit the shuttle, Piddu also shuffled two steps behind her, nodding his head. She would lunge forward for a shot, and he would lunged too, half a second late, almost tripping over her shoe.

"Move, Piddu!" Aparna snapped, smashing a clean drop shot.

"Yes, yes, always after you, madam," Piddu grinned, bowing slightly like a filmi hero.

The whole crowd burst out laughing, even the referee almost choked on his whistle.

The referee's patience was cracking. First, he whistled sharply. Then, when Piddu tried to pick up a shuttle but bent down in slow motion right in Aparna's path, the man finally shouted, "Boy! Let her play!"

But Piddu didn't care. His game plan was clear, be Arjun from Mahabharat, forget the shuttle, stay within three inches of Aparna. If she went left, he went left. If she jumped, he half-jumped. Once, when Aparna smashed the shuttle beautifully, Piddu clapped mid-match and almost dropped his racket.

The points kept piling up, but only for the other side. Aparna was the lone warrior, running across the court, sweating, hitting, smashing, diving. Piddu was simply her shadow.

In fact, the whole match looked like singles—Aparna versus the opponents—with a bodyguard running around.

Two sets of 21 points which was supposed to take half an hour, got completed in just 10 mins with straight sets. Clean sweep.

The moment it ended, Aparna dropped her racket, face red with embarrassment. She shot Piddu a death stare and snapped,

"Next time, try breathing at home. Here, only shuttle matters."

Then she stormed off the court.

The referee, exhausted, muttered under his breath, "Worst doubles match of my career."

And us? We were rolling on the ground, laughing till our stomachs hurt.

Sandy started singing Hindi song

"Dhaal Gaya din TOK

Ho gayi raat TOK

Jane do TOK

Jana hai'

Even the referee hid a smile. Aparna's story with Piddu had ended faster than it started.

After Piddu's badminton disaster, we all went to see other matches around.

The next highlight of the day was Kabaddi.

And who else but our very own Sandy was leading Sardar House's team.

Now, if you've ever seen Sandy, you'd know why everyone had high hopes. Broad shoulders, heavy frame, and the kind of presence that made even the juniors move aside in corridors. If kabaddi needed one word, it was *Sandy*.

"Today," he declared while tying his shoes, "opponents will fly like kites."

We all cheered, half-believing, half-praying.

The referee whistled, and the kabaddi match began.

Our Sardar House team looked solid in the opening minutes. One by one, they caught the opponent raiders, dragging them down to the mat. The crowd shouted "Kabaddi, kabaddi!" in rhythm, clapping, stomping, turning the whole ground into a mini stadium.

But slowly, things went downhill. One teammate slipped. Another got tricked out. One more stepped on the line by mistake. Within minutes, our fortress was crumbling. And suddenly, only Sandy was left on the court.

"Bro.," Sam whispered, "this will be his epic moment."

The opponent raider came in, chanting "kabaddi… kabaddi…". But Sandy didn't flinch. He just glared, unmoving.

Then, in one quick lunge, the raider dashed towards him. And Sandy? He spread his arms wide and grabbed him—tight. Very tight. In fact, so tight that the poor boy's face started turning red. From the stands, it didn't look like kabaddi anymore.

The crowd erupted with laughter. Even the referee blew the whistle twice, unsure whether to stop the match.

The raider wriggled, twisted, tried to slip free. But Sandy's grip was iron. "You're not going anywhere," Sandy muttered.

And just when it looked like Sandy had him cornered, the boy gave one desperate push. Sandy's balance wobbled.

And… disaster.

He toppled like a tree in slow motion. '**Thud!**' The ground shook. The whole audience burst into laughter.

The raider escaped back to his side, safe. Whistle blew—point to them. Match over.

Sardar House lost.

We couldn't breathe from laughing.

"Our fortress collapsed!" I shouted.

"The mighty Sandy has fallen!" Piddu added, clutching his stomach.

Sandy got up, dusting his knees, face red not from injury but from embarrassment.

Now it's was time for Piddu to sing a song.

"Tum mote ho toh kya hua, par khote hoain,

Tum Kabaddi khel khel ke haare ho."

The crowd exploded again. Even PT sir hid his grin behind his whistle.

Sandy walked off the ground like a fallen king, while we laughed so hard that tears rolled down our cheeks.

Kabaddi was supposed to be our easy win. Instead, it became the funniest tragedy of Sports Day.

After all the matches throughout the day.

It was time for the last game of the Sports day, volleyball.

Sam and I were part of the volleyball game.

We qualified for the semifinals with Raman house team.

Volleyball was one game we actually knew a bit about. I usually held the front centre position, blocking smashes near the net. Sam preferred the back centre, good at lifting and serving. Together, we made a decent pair.

The first match was the semi-final against Raman House. The whistle blew, ball flew, and the game began.

Sam started strong. His service was sharp, the ball flying just over the net like a guided missile. Point after point, Raman House kids struggled. I was holding the net like my life depended on it, jumping, blocking, throwing my arms high. Every time their smasher came forward, I was right there"

We had taken the first set. The second set went even smoother. Sam was on fire, and I had managed to block two smashes that could've knocked out my teeth.

Final score: Sardar House 2 – Raman House 0.

We were in the finals!

Our gang was thrilled. Even Sandy, still sulking from kabaddi, stood up and shouted, "Yes! That's my team!" Piddu waved both hands as if he'd just won the lottery.

But the finals… the match was with Tagore house. And leading them was Kabir.

When I looked across the net, there he was—tall, confident, adjusting his jersey, spinning the ball casually in his hands. He looked ready, dangerous, and to make things worse, I spotted Gayatri sitting in the stands. She wasn't with us, she wasn't even neutral. She was cheering for Kabir

The first serve flew across, and the final had begun.

From the very start, Tagore House came at us like hungry wolves. Kabir, their star player, was smashing every chance he got. His jumps were sharp, his hands quick, and each shot landed like a hammer on our side of the court.

Still, we held on. Sam served beautifully, keeping us in the game. I blocked two early smashes at the net, and the crowd roared. For a moment, it felt like maybe, just maybe, we could actually pull this off.

But Kabir wasn't going easy. He was waiting for the smallest slip. When the ball came near me again, he leapt and smashed it so hard that I barely managed to raise my hands. It deflected from me, went straight outside the line. Their point.

The crowd erupted.

We fought hard, but the first set slipped away—9 to 11. Tagore House took the lead.

During the short break, Sam looked at me. "Don't lose hope, we still have one more."

I nodded.

Second set began. This time, Sam and I switched positions—I went to the back centre, Sam took the front. The plan was simple: let him handle the smashes, I'd cover the back and keep the game steady.

The set was tight. 3–3, then 5–5, then 6–6. Every point was a battle. Dust flew from the court, students screamed slogans, whistles echoed.

The ball came flying my way. I went for it but added a little extra push. It sailed just past the Tagore court's back line. Point to them. My mistake.

Suddenly Gayatry shouted,

"Who's gonna give points? Gopal! Gopal!

"Who's gonna win the match? Tagore! Tagore!

That hit me hard and for couple of second I was completely lost in that, Kabir smashed his serve with full power.

Thud.

The ball crashed straight onto my head. The force was very hard, the world spun. I rolled on the ground and got fainted there immediately. The noise of the crowd faded into a blur.

And then, darkness.

The match, the shouts, everything disappeared.

When I opened my eyes, the bright tube light above me hurt more than the smash on my head. For a few seconds, I didn't even know where I was.

The white walls, the smell of Dettol, and the sound of a ceiling fan told me—this was the school's first aid room.

I tried to move, but my head spun. My knees felt scraped, and my right hand had a fresh bandage. A dull ache throbbed all over my body.

"Relax, don't get up suddenly."

It was the school doctor, leaning over me with his stethoscope still hanging around his neck. "You had a shock from the fall. Nothing serious. Just bruises. Your body reacted to the sudden jerk, that's why you fainted."

I blinked around. To my left, the entire LLB gang was packed into the tiny room. Sam stood near my feet, arms folded, trying to look calm but his eyes gave him away. Sandy was still in his kabaddi jersey, chewing his lip. Piddu looked like he'd just returned from a funeral, his usual grin nowhere in sight. And beside them, quietly, was Nidhi.

The doctor handed me a medicine and a glass of water.

"Take this medicines and wait for half an hour, if you feel Dizzyness again, then call me or else you may leave after half an hour". He scribbled something on a slip and walked out, leaving us in silence.

I touched the bandage on my knee. "How long… was I out?"

"About forty-five minutes," Sam said softly.

My throat went dry. "And the match?"

Sam hesitated. Then he sighed. "After you fell, we lost control. Their smashes kept coming. We couldn't keep up. We lost [illegible] straight points."

I closed my eyes. Not from pain, but from that heavy sinking feeling. The final… gone. Our chance… gone.

Piddu tried to lighten the mood. "what's the big deal? Nobody remembers the score, but everyone will remember that you fainted like a hero. ."

The gang broke into small, tired smiles.

After half an hour, the doctor waved us off. "He's fine now. Just don't let him run around."

Run around? I could barely walk straight. My legs felt like lead. So I leaned on Piddu's shoulder as we made our way out of the first aid room.

The gang walked with me slowly towards the bus stop. Sam carried my bag. Piddu kept cracking lame jokes about how I should get a helmet before playing volleyball again. I smiled weakly and trying to laugh.

As we turned the corner, I heard loud laughter.

There, near the bus stop, was Kabir. Surrounded by his teammates, grinning, holding the winner's shield.

And next to him, Gayatri.

She was clapping, laughing we haven't seen in weeks.

My steps froze. Piddu tugged me forward, but I couldn't move.

The same girl who once shouted the loudest for us, who once sat under the neem tree with our gang, who once called us her friends. Now, she didn't even glance in our direction.

Sam muttered under his breath, "Let's go."

I nodded slowly.

As we walked past them, I lowered my head. Not because of the loss, not because of the pain in my knee. But because something far bigger had slipped away.

A true friendship.

It doesn't shatter with a loud bang. It doesn't scream when it dies. It just… fades. One small crack at a time, until suddenly you realise, it's gone.

Completely. To zero.

Which is why this Sports Day felt so strange. For years, it had always been about madness, running in the sun, tripping over shoes, pulling each other's legs. Winning and losing never really mattered. We laughed at defeats, we danced at silly victories. It was always about the gang. About being together.

But this year… it was different.

Piddu had his ten-minute love story with Aparna. Sandy had his kabaddi collapse. Sam and I fought like lions in volleyball, only to end up on the losing side. All of that was funny, memorable, worth teasing each other about for years.

Yet behind all the laughter, one truth stood quietly, a broken friendship.

I forced a smile at the gang. "So," I said, "Sports Day taught us something important."

They all looked at me.

"Not stamina. Not fitness. Definitely not discipline," I added, and for the first time that evening, they chuckled.

"What then?" Sandy asked.

I sighed. "It taught us how to laugh at ourselves… even when everything goes wrong."

The gang laughed properly this time, the heaviness lifting just a little. Piddu even started singing again, his usual off-tune nonsense. And just like that, we all felt lighter.

— The Explosive Exam Day —

Present Day- 2025

I felt the same sudden thud on my face, just like that day.

The feeling was so real, it pulled me out of my thoughts in a second.

I exhaled slowly and turned my eyes back to the bed.

The school T-shirt lay there, worn out but still full of memories.

For a while, I just looked at it, caught somewhere between a smile and silence.

Then I folded it neatly, placed it aside, and reached back into the wooden box.

My fingers touched something hard and rectangular, smooth at the edges, rough at the corners.

I pulled it out.

A pencil box.

The blue colour had dulled over the years, and the lid carried tiny scratches, like small scars of time.

Scribbled on it, in fading blue ink, were the words:

"Gopal, Class XII-C."

I traced the letters slowly with my fingertip.

The ink had almost disappeared, but I could still feel every curve of my handwriting, the uneven 'p', the shaky 'C'.

I ran my thumb over the lid again. My eyes grew wet.

I closed them, and the years began to fade away once more.

School days- 1996

In the morning it was economics test. It was pre-boards time.

All exams were done, one by one.

Only the Economics paper was left. After that, school attendance turned from compulsory to "come if you feel like it."

The subject that sounded big enough to scare everyone, but equally boring enough to make us sleep in class.

That morning the whole school looked like a fish market. Some kids were cramming various topics, others were chanting definitions like mantras.

I wasn't panicking much, but the air around me was full of stress. Every second person had underlined notes in fluorescent pink. Someone had brought their tuition notes. Someone else was trying to teach their friends.

And then came Sandy. He walked in with his head high and a strange confidence in his face.

Piddu and Sam followed close behind, whispering and giggling, though they looked nervous.

Piddu muttered, "Bro, I only remember half the syllabus. If the paper asks from the other half, I'm dead."

Sam popped a peanut into his mouth. "Relax. If you die, I'll eat your tiffin."

Sandy didn't even look at them. He just smiled, eyes shining. "Don't worry. I've got everything covered today."

Piddu blinked. "Everything? What do you mean?"

Sandy tapped his pocket mysteriously but said nothing.

I just sat there watching them, shaking my head. And somewhere in my heart I felt that today was not going to be a normal exam day

The bell rang. We marched into the classroom like soldiers. Only difference was, instead of guns, we carried geometry boxes and borrowed pens.

Question papers were handed out. Within ten seconds, a collective groan filled the room. It was the kind of groan that needed no words, it said, *"same old story, tough paper!"*

I looked at the first question. It was about "balance of payment disequilibrium." My brain went blank. Disequilibrium was not just in the paper, it was also in my mind.

Around me, students reacted in their own styles. Some bent their heads so low, that it looked like they were trying to kiss the desk. Some started praying silently, moving lips without sound.

One fellow immediately raised his hand to ask for extra sheets. He hadn't even written a single line yet, just a drama to boost confidence.

Yadav sir walked over, looked at his blank paper, and said, "Son, first write one full page. Then I'll give you ten extra sheets also. Forget extra sheets, right now even the margin line is empty."

The whole class chuckled under their breath, while that poor guy sank into his bench like a punctured football.

And then, there was Sandy. Our dear Sandy had come prepared, not with concepts, but with chits. Small, neatly folded slips of paper hidden inside his socks, pencil box, even in his shirt pocket. He looked like a mini library.

I caught him slipping one out carefully, acting like he was scratching his leg. His eyes were shining. You could tell he had been waiting all year for this moment.

Piddu, sitting two benches away, tried signalling something with his eyebrows. Sam coughed loudly to cover it up. It looked less like an exam hall and more like a badly rehearsed play.

I shook my head. Only Sandy could think of giving his "final performance" in front of Yadav sir, the strictest invigilator in school.

And then came the disaster.

Yadav sir's shadow fell right on his desk.

"Mr. Sandeep!" His voice cut through the silence like a chalk squeak on the blackboard.

Sandy froze. The chit was half sticking out, fluttering like it wanted to surrender itself.

Yadav sir slowly picked it up between two fingers, the way people pick up dead lizards.

"What is this?"

The whole class turned. Some students gasped though they had just seen a live crime scene. A few others smirked, secretly happy it wasn't them.

Sandy tried. "Sir… this is just rough paper… I was…."

Don't act smart. If you were this smart, you wouldn't need chits in the first place." Yadav sir slammed the chit on the desk.

His voice boomed across the hall. "Do you think I am blind? You are caught red handed!"

Then came the gyan.

"You are not only cheating the school, you are cheating yourself! This is not how exams are cleared. Life is not about shortcuts. You think success comes .from these small papers? No! Success comes from hard work, honesty, and discipline!"

The lecture went on for five minutes. Each line heavier than the last.

Sandy's confidence had vanished. He sat quietly, staring at the question paper as if it was written in Chinese.

By the time the bell was close, Sandy had managed just a handful of answers. The boy who had entered with chits left with nothing but fear.

The bell rang. Papers were collected. Students stumbled out of the hall, some smiling, most shaking their heads.

Sandy walked out slowly, face pale, lips pressed tight. He had written hardly half the paper. Everyone knew what that meant. he was staring at failure.

Piddu tried cheering him. "Don't worry yaar… maybe the examiner will give marks for handwriting?"

"Shut up," Sandy snapped. His eyes were burning. "I got humiliated in front of everyone. Yadav sir made me a joker."

Sam, never serious, said, "But you *were* a joker… caught with chits, first time in history!" He laughed. Bad timing.

Sandy grabbed Sam's collar, whispered, "Enough jokes. I'm not going to sit quietly. Sir wants to treat me like a thief? I'll show him what real trouble looks like."

Piddu blinked. "What do you mean?"

Sandy leaned closer. "Toilet. After lunch. We'll blast something big. Sutli bomb. Let the whole school remember today."

Both froze. Sam's grin disappeared. Piddu swallowed hard but nodded anyway. Boys and their ego, logic never stood a chance.

I overheard the plan while packing my bag. My stomach tightened. This wasn't just another prank. This was madness.

After lunch break, the boys' toilet turned into their secret headquarters.

Sandy shut the door with the seriousness of a gang leader. He pulled out a polythene bag from under his shirt. Inside were two fat sutli bombs. Along with them, a small agarbatti, their brilliant timer system.

Piddu's jaw dropped. "Arre… this looks like proper Diwali stock!"

"Of course," Sandy said proudly. "I got arranged it from Chintu firecracker shop. This will be louder than the whole assembly prayer."

Sam picked one up and whistled. "Bro, if this goes off, even Gandhiji's photo in the principal's room will shake."

They all giggled like idiots. But behind the giggles was fear. Hands trembled a little.

Sandy explained the plan. "We'll light the agarbatti, stick it near the bombs. It'll take five minutes to reach. By then we'll be back in class, acting innocent."

Piddu nodded like a soldier. "Yes, yes. Roger that"

I entered right then, breathless. "Are you mad? Do you want the police to come? Stop this nonsense before someone gets hurt!"

Sandy rolled his eyes. "Relax, Gopal. It's just for fun. A blast, some smoke, nothing else. Don't act like our father."

I argued, begged, even scolded. But Sandy was determined. Sam laughed at my worried face. Piddu added filmy dialogue: "In friendship, a little risk is compulsory."

I tried the calm voice first. "Listen, this is wrong. People can get hurt. Even if it's small, someone can panic."

Sandy laughed, short and cold. "Gopal, chill. If you're scared, fine. Just don't stand in our way."

"And if you get caught? Then what?" I said, staring at them.

Sam shrugged. "Worst case, we get suspension. Best case, we get fame. Either way, we win."

I walked around the toilet "Do you know what suspension means? Your parents will come. They'll be angry. Principal will never look the same. What if someone faints? What if a small kid gets hurt? You think it's just a story then?"

Sandy's eyes went hard. "You don't get it. Yadav sir made me a fool, slapped my pride. I want them to feel that shame today. The school will speak of this for years."

"By hurting others?" I said. "Is that revenge or childishness?"

Sam, who always sounded like he had swallowed confidence, leaned in. "Bro, stop acting scared. You always run away when it's fun. Don't start your coward routine again." The guilt pressed down harder than I expected.

I hit back with reason. "Fun doesn't include smoke and bombs. Fun doesn't include hospital rooms. It's not clever. It's dangerous."

They exchanged looks. A long pause. For a heartbeat, I thought maybe they would see sense.

Then Sandy picked up a bomb, grinned, and said softly, "We light it. We run. Five minutes. No one gets hurt. Are you in or out?"

I imagined my parents' faces. I imagined Yadav sir's disappointed glare. I imagined someone elderly coughing in the corridor. The images sat heavy in my chest.

I sighed and swallowed the truth I wanted to keep. "I am out."

Sam already had the matchbox out. Sandy struck the match with a steady hand. The agarbatti caught flame, faint and orange.

They set the agarbatti near the sutli bombs. It smelled faintly of incense mixed with something sharp. Five minutes. That was the countdown.

They ran out like schoolboys playing hide-and-seek. I stood frozen, my legs weak. For a moment, I wanted to snatch the bombs and throw them away. I didn't.

I turned and walked out of the toilet into the bright corridor. My chest felt hollow. I had tried but it was not enough.

We spilled back into class like nothing had happened. Some students chatted. Some looked nervous. The exam room smelled of ink and defeat.

I sat down and opened my bag. That's when I noticed. My pencil box was missing. My heart dropped.

It wasn't just any box. It had my name written in blue marker, *Gopal class XII C*, it was like seeing my own fingerprint at a crime scene.

For a second I thought I'd left it in the exam hall. I stood up, calm at first. "Maybe I kept it in the bench," I told myself.

I searched everywhere but couldn't find it. My worry spiked, it must have fallen in the toilet while I was coming out.

I ran towards the toilet. My legs felt too heavy and then too fast. The corridor blurred. Teachers shouted, "Don't run!", but their voices were far away. My mind repeated the name on the box like a prayer. *Gopal. Gopal. Gopal.*

Before I could reach the toilet door, it happened.

A sound ripped through the corridor. Not just loud, it punched your chest before it even reached your ears.

From the toilet side, small pieces of plaster had fallen. A cracked mirror hung like it was about to fall. The smell of burnt powder mixed with phenyl made the whole corridor stink like Diwali gone wrong.

Teachers rushed in, shouting for order. "Don't run! Stay calm!" Which, of course, made everyone run faster and scream louder.

I stood frozen, heart hammering against my ribs. The blast site was just metres away, and my pencil box was still inside. My name. My handwriting. My future, lying in that smoke.

Meanwhile, Sandy, Piddu, and Sam dragged themselves back to their desk. They exchanged quick glances that said, 'Mission successful'.

I wanted to shout, to run, to disappear. But my legs carried me back to class, where I sat coughing, eyes watering, praying no one had seen me near the toilet.

Because once that smoke cleared, the evidence would point only one way. Straight at me.

The smoke had barely thinned when the sound of heels echoed in the corridor. Everyone went silent. Only one person in the whole school could make silence this heavy.

The Principal .

She stormed in, followed by two teachers, her face tight with anger.

She stepped inside, scanning the rows. "Where is Gopal?"

My heart stopped. For a second, I thought maybe I had misheard. But no, she said it again, louder this time. "Gopal, stand up!"

My legs felt like stone as I rose. Every pair of eyes drilled into me. She didn't wait. "Come with me."

The walk to her cabin felt like walking straight into a courtroom where the verdict was already decided. Inside, she shut the door with a bang. I could barely breathe.

She slapped me. Once, twice, my cheeks burning. "How dare you?" she shouted. "You planted bombs in the toilet? Are you trying to blow up the school?"

"No, madam!" I cried. "I didn't do it!"

Her hand slammed on the table. "Then explain how your pencil box was found there. With your name written on it!"

I stammered. "Madam, I… I had gone to pee… I must have forgotten it there."

"Rubbish!" she snapped. "You expect me to believe such a lie?"

Before I could answer, Yadav sir entered. His voice was softer. "Madam, I know Gopal. He's not that kind of boy. He doesn't do this sort of mischief. We should find the real culprits."

She turned to him, furious. "So what do you suggest? Ignore the evidence? His pencil box is proof enough!"

Yadav sir looked at me, eyes heavy. "Then tell us, Gopal. Who was with you? Who else did this?"

I shook my head, tears rolling. "I don't know, sir."

Madam's voice cut through again. "Call his father. And prepare his rustication letter. He doesn't deserve to be in this school."

My knees went weak. I dropped down, touched her feet. "Please, madam. Don't call my parents. Don't do this. I didn't do it, I swear."

I knelt there, tears rolling, my palms pressed to the cold floor. My cheek still burned from her slaps.

"Who did it, Gopal?" Yadav sir's voice was calmer, but it carried weight. "We know you are not that kind of boy. Tell us the names."

I shook my head, choking on words. "I don't know, sir… please believe me."

Madam snapped, "Stop wasting our time! You think this is a joke? You think we will let bombs blast inside our school? Either you speak now, or I call your father and hand you the rustication letter. Decide!"

Rustication. The word felt like death. I imagined my father walking into school, his face pale with shame. My mother crying, neighbours whispering. The thought was worse than any slap.

I sobbed harder. "Please madam… don't call my parents… I swear I didn't do it…"

"Then who did?" Yadav sir said again, softer this time. He leaned forward. "Save yourself, Gopal. Tell us."

Something inside me cracked, and the words burst out before I could stop them. "It was Sandy… and Piddu… and Sam. They lit the bombs, not me." My voice broke, rising louder as tears spilled.

The room went quiet.

Madam leaned back in her chair, eyes sharp. "I knew it," she said. "Call the three of them here right now. And inform their parents to come immediately."

Yadav sir nodded to the peon at the door. Then he looked at me with a kind of sadness. "Go back to class, Gopal."

I stood up on weak legs, wiping my face. Relief and guilt wrestled inside me. I had spoken the truth, but it felt like betrayal. My voice still echoed in my head: *It was Sandy, and Piddu, and Sam.*

And I knew, when they found out, nothing between us would ever be the same.

By the time I returned to class, the news had already spread like fire in a cracker factory.

Everyone was whispering, glancing at me. I sat at my desk, silent, staring at my shoes.

Sandy, Piddu, and Sam were already called to the office. Their parents came soon after, rushing in with tense faces.

I lingered near the corridor just to hear bits of what was happening inside. Voices rose, muffled but sharp. Madam's voice carried above all. "Your sons have disgraced the school. This is criminal behaviour. If we wished, we could file a police complaint."

There was pleading, arguing, even a chair scraping against the floor. The whole meeting stretched for more than an hour. Every minute, my chest felt heavier.

Finally, the door opened. The three boys came out, eyes down, their parents dragging them like culprits from a police van. Madam had spared them expulsion, only suspension till the final board exams, with a final warning.

I waited near the exit, wanting to explain myself. To tell Sandy that I hadn't wanted to speak, that I had been forced. That I was sorry.

But before I could open my mouth, Sandy grabbed my collar with one hand and pushed me against the wall. His eyes were red, his voice low and shaking. "Don't ever come in front of me again. Or I'll smash your face."

He shoved me back, hard enough to sting, then walked off without looking again. Piddu and Sam followed, both glaring at me like strangers.

And just like that, the LLB gang was gone. Suspended by the school, broken by anger, and for me, lost forever.

That evening, I walked to the bus stop slower than usual. For the first time, I was alone, no Gayatri beside me, no LLB gang around me. Just me and my heavy steps.

I kept replaying the cabin scene. My voice breaking, naming them. Their parents' faces. The anger in Sandy's eyes. Somewhere I knew I had no choice. If I had stayed quiet, I'd be the one thrown out. But knowing that didn't make it hurt any less.

That night, I sat with my pencil box in front of me. Same dent, same stickers, same name written in blue marker. It looked innocent, but it had turned into a weapon that ended a friendship.

Maybe that's how school life is. Friendships begin over shared samosas and silly jokes. And sometimes, they end over a single mistake that nobody can take back.

For me, the chapter of the LLB gang had closed. No last joke, no final hug, No farewells. Just silence that stayed.

Friendships don't always end with fights. Sometimes, they end with silence... and a name written in blue marker.

Mother's intuition

Present Day- 2025

This time, I couldn't control my tears.

One after another, they rolled down my cheeks, warm and quiet, the kind that don't make a sound but say everything.

I wiped them with the back of my hand and took a slow breath.

No matter how strong you think you've become, some memories still find their way through the cracks.

I looked at the wooden box again.

It just sat there on the bed, calm, patient, waiting for me to open another corner of my past.

I reached inside once more, my fingers brushing through the old papers and photos, until they touched something soft.

I pulled it out carefully.

It was a shirt, once white, now closer to off-white, carrying stains not of food or ink, but of time and memory.

Written all across it, in blue and black pens, were the voices of my classmates, frozen forever in ink.

"Wish you all the best."

"You are really a GEM."

"I will miss you."

Some letters were bold, some uneven, some fading away, but every single one felt alive.

I smiled through the tears that refused to stop.

That's the thing about school goodbyes, you never really leave them behind; you just carry them quietly, folded like this shirt, tucked away somewhere in your heart.

School days- 1996

After the pre-board exams, the school became like a government office, open, but nobody really cared if you showed up. They told us, "You can come if you want, otherwise prepare at home." Which was a polite way of saying, "We've done our part, now you suffer alone."

Most students, including me, chose the second option. Why sit in an empty classroom pretending to study, when you could sit at home and study on your bed. And honestly, after *that* incident, I didn't feel like stepping into school again. Every corner of that building reminded me of something I didn't want to remember.

Friendships are finished. Over.

Gayatri stopped talking, and the LLB gang also kept their distance from me.

Only one voice still reached me, Nidhi. Every two-three days, the landline would ring, and it would be her. She'd start with casual chit-chat. "Did you study?" "This accountancy problem is killing me." "Why is economics so cruel?" But between her words, I could always sense she was checking up on me, making sure I wasn't drifting too far into my own silence.

And I must admit, those calls were my oxygen cylinders. Even if we only talked about boring things like syllabus, I felt a little human again after speaking to her. Otherwise, my days were long, stretched like old chewing gum.

It had been almost a month since I last spoke to any of the LLB gang. My room had become my world, and my books my roommates. The house was quieter too. Maa and Papa had noticed. Earlier, the phone used to ring at least once or twice daily, and I'd lock myself in the room, laughing, shouting, sometimes fighting with friends on the landline. Now, the phone sat there like an unused showpiece. And me… like a ghost haunting my own house.

One late evening, after finishing dinner, I was in my room, studying economics. The house was quiet, just the faint noise of TV from the living room.

And then, *tring tring*. The landline phone rang. That sharp metallic sound echoed through the house.

"Gopal, your phone!" Maa shouted, her voice travelling through the closed door.

"Coming, Maa," I replied, my heart already guessing who it might be.

I picked up the receiver.

"Hello?"

"Hey Gopal! How are you?" a familiar cheerful voice rang on the other end.

I smiled unconsciously. "Hey Nidhi… I'm good yaar. How about you? How's the study going?"

"Going okay," she sighed dramatically. "But this economics sucks."

"I know," I laughed, finally relaxing. "Every time I read the law of marginal utility, I remember Sandy's explanation."

We both chuckled, but my laughter ended abruptly, like someone had pressed pause. For a few seconds, silence filled the line. The kind that reminds you of everything you've lost.

Nidhi broke it gently. "Anyways… what's the plan for tomorrow?"

"Tomorrow?" I asked, pretending to think. "Nothing special. Same boring routine of study."

"You forgot or what? Tomorrow is our class XII farewell day at school!" Her voice was bubbling with excitement.

"Is it?" I scratched my head, though she couldn't see it. "I completely forgot. But it doesn't matter… I'm not coming. Better to stay home and study."

"Come on, Gopal," she said softly, her voice dipping. "I know what's going on in your mind. But it's our last day as students. After this, who knows when we'll all be together again? Everyone will take their own path. We can't miss this."

I swallowed hard. "You know what happened these past weeks. I don't feel like coming. Everything will come alive again… and it'll mess with my head. It'll ruin my studies." My voice was heavy, even to my own ears.

"Please Gopal… for me, come. It's our last day." This time her tone cracked a little, her emotions spilling through.

I closed my eyes. I wanted to say yes, but my heart was still a mess. "Calm down, Nidhi… let me think. But I'm not sure."

"Gopal, please…" She almost pleaded now.

I stayed silent for a few seconds, then forced myself to end it. "Nidhi, I'll think about it. Chal… bye."

I kept staring at the receiver in my hand, even after the line went dead. My eyes burned, and I could feel them getting wet.

I placed the receiver down slowly and just stood there, staring at it like it had betrayed me.

A gentle hand touched my back. I turned, and Maa was there, holding a glass of water.

"Have it, Gopal," she said softly. "Come sit with us, watch TV for a while. You'll feel better."

I avoided her eyes. "It's nothing, Maa."

She smiled faintly, the kind of smile that says, *don't try to fool me, beta.*

"I can understand everything. Gayatri and your gang friends… they suddenly stopped calling you. Earlier, every day, you used to get one or two phone calls. You would laugh, argue, talk for hours. Now both you and the phone… very quiet." Her eyes glistened as she said it.

That broke something in me. I couldn't hold it anymore. I hugged her tightly, my voice shaking.

"I lost my friends, Maa. I lost my friends."

And then the tears came, like a flood I couldn't stop. I cried for two minutes straight, like a child again. Maa just kept patting my back, her own eyes moist, but steady. From the corner of my eye, I saw Papa's shadow in the doorway. But Maa gave him a small signal to stay back.

After a while, she cupped my face in her hands. "Beta, sharing makes you lighter. Maybe you'll even find some answers."

I wiped my nose clumsily. "Maa… can we sit in my room and talk?"

She nodded. We went inside. I lay down, resting my head on her lap like I used to when I was small. Her fingers gently moved through my hair, and for the first time in weeks, I felt my chest loosen a little.

Slowly, I told her everything, the last few weeks, the incident, how the LLB gang broke, how Gayatri turned away, how I felt like a stranger in my own school.

She listened without interrupting, only nodding, only stroking my head. When I was done, she finally spoke.

"Beta, in friendship, nobody is right or wrong. If you start judging whose fault it is, then it's no longer friendship. Sometimes situations create distance, sometimes misunderstandings pile up. But if the bond is real, it doesn't break… it only bends. And time, slowly, straightens it again. You just have to be patient."

She paused, looking into my eyes. "I know it hurts when the people you laughed with every day suddenly stop talking. When the same voices that filled your evenings with jokes and secrets now go silent. But that silence doesn't mean friendship is gone. Sometimes people get carried away, sometimes ego comes in the way, sometimes they don't even realise how much they're hurting the other person."

Her hand pressed gently on my chest. "You feel empty now because those friends were a part of you. Losing them feels like losing yourself. But beta, real friendship is never one incident, one fight, or one mistake. If it was strong once, it will find its way back. Don't bury yourself under the weight of what went wrong. Keep the door open. Let time do its work."

I felt my throat tighten again, but this time not with tears, with a strange kind of relief. Like someone had just told me it wasn't the end of the world.

I sat up a little, looking at her. She continued, her voice firm but gentle.

She wiped the corner of my eye with her pallu and said softly,

"And listen carefully, beta… avoiding something never solves it. It only makes the wound grow deeper. The more you hide from it, the more it will control you. Every time you think of school, you'll feel the same heaviness. Is that what you want?"

I looked away, but she tilted my face back towards her.

"The only way is to face it. Not to prove anyone wrong, not to win anything, just to free yourself. If you go tomorrow, you'll see… maybe they still don't talk, maybe nothing changes. But at least you won't be running away. You'll stand there with your head high, and that will give you peace."

She took a deep breath, her voice firm now.

"Tomorrow is your last day in that school, Gopal. If you skip it, that regret will follow you for years. But if you go, you will carry memories instead of emptiness. And believe me, one day when you look back, it won't be the silence you remember… it will be the laughter, the faces, the moments you lived together. That's what you will cherish all your life."

Her words landed like cool water on burning skin. For weeks, I had been carrying this load. And in that one moment, it felt like someone opened a soda bottle, *fizz!*, the pressure released.

She smiled, brushing my hair back. "Now go. Call Nidhi. Tell her you're coming."

I hesitated for a second, then picked up the receiver. My fingers trembled slightly as I dialled her number.

"Hello Aunty, Namaste," I said when her mother picked up. "Sorry to disturb you… can I speak to Nidhi?"

Within seconds, her excited voice burst on the line. "Hello! Gopal?"

I took a deep breath, this time my voice steady. "Hey Nidhi… I'm coming tomorrow. See you at school."

For a moment, there was silence, and then she screamed, "Yaaayyy! Gopal, I'm so happy! Finally! Okay okay, see you tomorrow. Bye and good night."

Before I could even reply, she cut the call in her excitement.

I slowly kept the receiver back. When I turned, Maa was standing there at the doorway. She didn't say a word. She just smiled. I smiled back and nodded.

I don't know why, but mothers have this god-gifted intuition. They know what's running in our minds even before we admit it to ourselves. They pick up the smallest changes, the slightest silences. Maybe that's why we say God couldn't be everywhere, so he created Maa.

That night, for the first time in weeks, I slept without the heavy stone pressing on my chest. Tomorrow was waiting.

— Those Days, That Last Bell —

Morning of farewell day.

It felt heavier than even exam mornings. Today it was a strange mix of excitement, sadness, and that weird nervousness you get before the Economics exams.

The road to school also looked different. Today my legs felt heavy in a different way.

Finally, I reached the school gate. For two minutes, I just stood there, staring at it. My heart was saying, "Go in." My mind was saying, "Should I?" It felt like both were pulling me from opposite sides.

In the end, I stepped in.

Corridor looked almost empty. Usually, the morning is full of noise, shouts. Today, there was silence. I walked slowly to my class.

When I pushed myself inside the class room, a wave of awkwardness hit me. I went straight to my desk and sat quietly. My eyes were scanning the room, but my body was stiff, like I had entered a stranger's house.

Inside my head, one thought was hammering, *How will everyone look at me after that last incident? Will they talk? Will they taunt?*

But then Ashu walked in. He looked at me, smiled and said,

"Hey bro, how are you? How's studies going on?"

That's it. Simple, normal, like nothing ever happened. I smiled weakly, nodded.

Then Ravi walked in with his usual energy. He patted my shoulder and said,

"Gopal! during pre-board exam you looked like you were studying for UPSC. And today you are so serious like it's your wedding."

Everyone around laughed.

And in that moment, something clicked in my head. Maybe Maa was right. Maybe I was carrying unnecessary baggage. Maybe nobody really cared as much as I thought.

I took a deep breath.

But then, my eyes went to Sandy's desk. Empty. Piddu's desk. Empty. Sam's desk. Empty. It hit me suddenly, they're suspended till the exam. They won't come today. A wave of fear went through me. *Does this mean… I won't even get to meet them one last time?*

I felt my throat tighten.

Just then, Nidhi walked in. Straight to me. No hesitation. Sat right next to me with a smile. "So, Mr. Serious, stop overthinking. Just enjoy the day."

I gave a weak smile. She leaned closer.

"Listen, nobody remembers what happened that day. Trust me, everyone's busy with their own emotions. Stop acting like you're carrying the whole world on your shoulders."

I kept quiet, still lost in thoughts. She nudged me with her elbow.

"At least smile for the photos today, right now you look like you have a constipation."

I laughed a little, shaking my head.

She continued, "See, look around. No books, no homework. Just cameras, pens, and memories."

Her voice had that ease which made me feel… lighter.

But my eyes searched again, this time for Gayatri. She wasn't there. My brain, of course, started a marathon of questions. Is she with Kabir? Will she come later? Or maybe she won't come at all?

I shook my head, but the thoughts kept running.

More students entered, and the whole classroom started filling up. But it wasn't the same as every day. No heavy bags. No textbooks. No homework pressure. Instead, everyone had only two things: ink pens and cameras.

The air itself felt different, half excitement, half silence.

One corner, someone was clicking pictures. Another corner, two friends were writing notes for each other. Some people were just staring at the blackboard as if it was suddenly a piece of history. And a few… already looked emotional, wiping their eyes.

It was strange. The same classroom, same desks, same walls. But today, it felt like we were standing inside a memory, not a classroom.

An announcement came from the mic, "All class XII students, please gather near the podium."

We walked out slowly. The whole school ground felt different today. Not like Sports Day noise, not like Assembly silence. It was something in between, heavy yet cheerful.

Principal Madam walked up to the stage. Normally, her face is serious, like she's about to announce a new set of rules. But today, she started with a big smile. That itself shocked half the crowd.

She looked at us and said,

"You are a very brilliant batch. But also… very notorious."

Everyone laughed. She continued,

"We saw students with exceptional talent, who made the name of KVS shine. And we also had students who always kept us on our toes. At that time they made us angry, but later when we remember those moments… they make us laugh."

We all looked at each other, half embarrassed, half proud.

Then Madam's tone softened.

"You are leaving school now. Ahead of you is a new life, full of chances and dreams. Some days will be tough, but many days will be beautiful. I have full faith… you will shine. Each one of you has something special. Don't forget that."

She paused for a moment, her eyes scanning the crowd.

"Remember...Marks are important, but they are not everything. What matters is honesty, kindness, and hard work. Carry these with you. Success will follow."

The ground went silent. Even the backbenchers, who usually talk non-stop, were quiet.

And then she smiled again.

"Best of luck to all of you. Wherever you go, whatever you become… always make your school proud. And don't forget us teachers when you achieve big things. We'll be waiting to hear your names."

For a second, nobody clapped. We were just stunned that Madam was being so light and emotional. Then suddenly a few boys whistled. In front of the Principal! And the best part, she laughed and clapped with us.

That smile on her face… I knew all of us would remember it forever.

Then came the real surprise. "Now I invite Nidhi, class XII-C, to share a few words on behalf of the students."

We all turned to look at her. Nidhi walked to the mic with a calm smile, but I could see her hands were shaking a little.

She began softly,

"On the first day of class XII, some of us were old friends, some were strangers. In one year, all those lines disappeared. Today we are all one family."

She paused, took a breath, then continued,

"We had our own silly stories… PT periods under the hot sun."

Half the ground groaned in unison. Someone shouted, "And no water after running!" Laughter spread, even PT sir shook his head with a grin.

"Those long boring assemblies where we only counted minutes."

The whole crowd clapped and laughed. Even Principal Madam laughed and joined in, clapping along with us. That was the first time we saw her openly admit assemblies were boring too. The cheer that followed was louder than any assembly prayer ever had been.

"Sharing tiffins in the middle of economics class."

At that, a loud cheer went up. "Yes!" one boy shouted, holding up his hand like he was showing proof. Even the economics teacher smiled and nodded, she knew exactly who was always caught eating.

"Our mass bunk for a movie."

Someone yelled, "Best day ever!"

Yadav Sir immediately shouted from the teachers' side, "Rangeela, right?"

We all froze for a second, shocked. Then the ground exploded with whistles and claps. We couldn't believe they knew all along, and yet never complained. The laughter on Yadav Sir's face was unforgettable, like he had been waiting years to say this.

"Chauhan sir's terror."

Instant reaction, students groaned, teachers laughed, and even Chauhan sir himself smiled but pointed his finger as if saying, "Careful!" Everyone laughed louder.

"PT sir's dance motivation."

The students started clapping in rhythm, a few even shouted "Tunak Tunak Tun!" PT sir waved his hand like a hero, laughing.

"The fights, the crushes, the punishments, and those last-minute exam panics."

That line hit both ways, everyone laughed at the word 'crushes', a few hooted, while others went quiet, suddenly thinking of their own secret stories.

Teachers looked at each other knowingly, as if saying, "Yes, we always knew."

And when she said, "last-minute exam panics," the ground shook with applause, because every single one of us had lived that moment.

By then, the whole atmosphere was electric. Some were laughing, some were hiding tears, and for the first time, it felt like both students and teachers were part of the same big inside joke.

Her voice cracked a little at the end,

"All of these moments… they made this one year unforgettable."

She paused for a moment, looking at all of us. Her eyes were shiny now.

"We fought, we teased each other, sometimes we even stopped talking for days. But in the end, we always came back together. That is what made us family."

The ground was silent. You could actually hear a few people sniffing.

She took a deep breath and smiled softly,

"After today, we may not sit in the same class again.

We may not hear the same bell ringing for lunch.

We may not hide notebooks before surprise tests.

But I know, in our hearts, this school and these memories will always stay with us."

By now, half the students had watery eyes. Even a few teachers were wiping their glasses.

"And when we meet again, maybe years later… I hope we still laugh at the same silly stories. I hope we still remember each other not by marks or ranks, but by the moments we shared."

She paused, wiped her eyes quickly, and then added,

"And a very big thank you to all our teachers… for scolding us, guiding us, and never giving up on us, even when we were impossible to handle."

The teachers at the back smiled, some clapped softly.

Nidhi looked towards the stage, her voice trembling,

"And thank you, Principal Madam… for being strict when we needed discipline, and kind when we needed support. We will always carry your blessings with us."

Her voice broke fully on the last line,

"Thank you… for being good friends, for the strength of each other, and for being a family. We will miss this school, teachers, everyone.

The words were simple, but they hit hard. The students clapped, whistles, some shouted "Thank you Nidhi!", while the teachers looked at each other and smiled with pride. Even Principal Madam nodded, her eyes softer than we had ever seen before.

I don't remember if we clapped or cried first. Probably both at the same time.

The moment Nidhi stepped down from the stage, the farewell sort of began right there. Nobody waited to go back to the classroom.

One group started clapping, another group started hugging. Soon it spread everywhere, people rushing towards their friends, arms wide open. Boys who never hugged anyone suddenly became emotional wrestlers. Girls who used to fight over seats were crying together, holding hands.

It was chaos, but the sweetest kind.

Best friends hugged and promised, "We'll never forget each other." But deep down, everyone knew, life changes. Still, in that moment, those promises felt real.

Some students were crying openly, tears rolling down their cheeks. Others were hiding their faces, pretending to laugh. Even the "tough guys", the ones who always acted like heroes, were quietly wiping their eyes when nobody was watching.

Teachers stood a little apart, watching us like parents at a wedding. They didn't stop us, didn't scold. They just smiled, some with proud faces, some with watery eyes.

It felt like time had slowed down, just hugs, laughter, tears, and voices echoing across the school ground.

Soon the hugs turned into a new craze, shirts.

White shirts that had looked neat in the morning slowly became graffiti walls.

It started with one boy pulling out a pen and writing on his friend's back, "Best of luck, bro." In two minutes, the whole ground was filled with people turning around, asking autographs.

Messages popped up everywhere:

"Don't forget me."

"You are the laziest person I ever met."

"The best person I ever met."

Some didn't write words, they made doodles, moustaches, hearts, random cartoons.

But nobody said anything out loud. The ink was enough.

Every shirt slowly turned into a memory book. The kind you could fold, keep in a cupboard, and open years later to cry and laugh at the same time.

In the middle of it all, one joker shouted, "Arre, don't sign too big. I need space for 20 more people!" Everyone laughed and pushed each other to get their turn.

The air smelled of ink, sweat, and emotions. By then, nobody cared about neatness, nobody cared about stains. We just wanted to leave a mark, a proof that we were here, together, once.

After all the laughter, hugs, and signatures, something inside me felt heavy again.

I slipped away quietly from the crowd and walked back to the classroom.

The room was empty now. Silent. Just me and the four walls that had seen everything, fights, jokes, punishments, secrets.

I went straight to my desk. My eyes fell on it, my name carved roughly on the corner, and right in the middle, the words: *LLB Property*.

That hit me like a punch. I put my hands on the desk, bent down, and tears started rolling. I hid my face in my hands and cried softly.

For a while, there was only the sound of my own breath.

Then the door creaked open. Footsteps.

"Gopal," a soft voice called. It was Nidhi.

I didn't lift my head. I didn't want her to see my face.

She tried to lighten the moment, "Look who's here."

Another voice followed. "Gopal…"

That voice I knew instantly. Gayatri.

Still, I kept my head down.

The room went silent for a few seconds. My heart was racing.

Then Gayatri spoke slowly, her voice trembling,

"Gopal… I had to make a choice. Between friendship… and relationship. I made my choice."

Her words cut through me. It felt like someone had pulled the floor from under my feet.

My hands pressed harder against my face. I wanted to look up. I wanted to ask her why. I wanted to tell her I still value friendship more than anything. But the memory of that day came rushing back like a storm, the shouts, the blame, the pain. My throat locked. My voice betrayed me.

I heard her place something on the desk. Then their footsteps moved towards the door. Both left quietly.

The room felt colder now. The silence heavier. I wanted to run after them, talk, fix everything.

But instead, I sat there crying harder, my head still buried in my hands.

I was still sitting with my head down, eyes wet, when I heard the door creak again. Footsteps entered the room.

"Gopal," a gentle voice called. It was Nidhi again.

Without looking up, I said softly, "Nidhi… please, can you leave me alone for some time?"

There was silence for a second. I thought she had left.

Then another voice came, full of mischief,

"Stand up, my friend. Otherwise Sandy's dog 'Pluto', from the Tailor's bedsheet, will bite you on your backside."

I froze. That voice. I knew it.

I looked up in shock, and there they were. Piddu. Sam. And Sandy. Standing right in front of me with wide grins.

Tears rolled again, this time faster. The only word that slipped out of my mouth was,

"Sorry… I'm so sorry, guys. Because of me….."

Before I could finish, Sandy came forward and hugged me tight.

"*Koi baat nahi, yaar. Forget it.*"

Piddu patted my back, "Nidhi told us everything. We know why you said our names that day. If we were in your place, we might have done the same."

I blinked, confused. "But… how come you guys are here? You were suspended."

Sam grinned. "Suspended? Arre, our parents wrote apology letters the very next day. Principal Madam never even issued the suspension letter."

Sandy winked, "So officially, we were never suspended. Surprise!"

I didn't know whether to laugh or cry. Maybe both. I pulled all three into a hug, and for the first time in weeks, I felt light.

We took out pens and signed on each other's shirts, laughed at our old silly fights, and cracked jokes. Piddu borrowed Ashu's camera and clicked a group photo, four idiots standing together, trying to look serious but failing because of our stupid grins.

For a moment, it felt like nothing had ever gone wrong. We were back. The LLB gang.

By the time we stopped laughing and wiping our eyes, the farewell program was already over. Students had started leaving, carrying their ink-covered shirts and watery eyes.

We looked at each other, and Sandy said, "Enough emotional drama, let's have one last samosa?"

There was only one answer. All of us shouted, "Krishna Samosa Centre!"

That place had been our adda for years. Half our pocket money had gone into samosas and chai there. If our school was our second home, Krishna's samosa stall was our third.

We moved out of the class, still laughing through our tears. Suddenly Sandy stopped, turned around, and shouted,

"Guys, let's see our renovated Toilet room… haannnnnnn!"

For a second we just stared, then Piddu raised his hands dramatically and declared,

"Last loo on the last day!"

That was enough. All of us burst out laughing and ran towards the toilet like it was some picnic spot. Other students passing by must have thought we had lost our minds.

Inside, we inspected it like engineers. "Arre wah, new tiles!" Sam said, running his hand across the wall. Sandy pointed at the new flush tank and went, "VIP treatment, boys." Even in that silly place, we were laughing so hard our stomachs hurt.

After the "loo program," we stepped out, ready to leave. But Sandy suddenly stopped us again.

"Wait a minute, guys. Let's mark our place here."

He pulled out a black marker from his pocket, God knows why he even had one. He went straight to the spot where he had once placed that infamous *sutli bomb*. Carefully, he bent down and wrote on the wall:

"With love, from LLB gang."

We all stood there watching. None of us said anything for a few seconds. That small line on the wall... it wasn't just words. It was our stamp. Our proof. Our madness carved into history.

Piddu finally broke the silence, "One day, when juniors see this, they'll wonder who the idiots were."

Sandy grinned, "And that's exactly how legends are born."

We all laughed again, but somewhere deep inside, we knew, this was the last time we would be doing such madness together.

We walked out together towards the exit, our shirts full of ink, our hearts full of memories.

We all stood for a second, turned around, and looked at the school building. For a few seconds, nobody spoke.

Then Piddu broke the silence with his classic one-liner while pointing his figure towards the building, "If we pass, we won't meet again. If we fail, then we'll meet again."

For two seconds we stared at him, then burst out laughing. That was Piddu, turning even a farewell into a joke. But deep inside, we all knew... whether we passed or failed, life would never bring back these same days.

We started our walk again, as we crossed the gate, I slipped my hand into my pocket and felt something. A small envelope. I pulled it out.

On the front, it was written in Gayatri's handwriting: "To GEM", but the word *GEM* had been struck off with a single line. Just below it, she had written softly, *"Gopal."*

That one scratched-out word hit harder than the whole letter inside.

My throat tightened. I opened it carefully. Inside, a small card.

"Thank you for everything, Gopal. Wish you all the best. I wish things could have been different. - Gayatri."

I didn't react much. I just folded the card back, put it in the envelope, and slipped it into my pocket again. Some feelings are too heavy to show in front of friends.

The four of us stepped out, heading towards Krishna Samosa Centre. We didn't talk about the future. We didn't talk about what would happen tomorrow. We just talked nonsense, cracked jokes, and pretended this wasn't the end.

The samosa party was over. It was time to move towards home.

We crossed the road together, laughing, teasing, pretending like nothing would ever change. But somewhere inside, we all knew this was it.

At the corner, we stopped. No more words left. Just one last round of hugs. One last pat on the back. One last smile through wet eyes.

We finally departed with a final goodbye and a final hug.

Maa's words echoed in my head while sitting in the bus.

"*Tomorrow is your last day in that school, Gopal. If you skip it, this regret will follow you for years. But if you go, you will carry memories instead of emptiness. And believe me, one day when you look back, it won't be the silence you remember… it will be the laughter, the faces, the moments you lived together.*"

I smiled faintly, whispering in my heart, "*Thanks, Maa.*"

Maybe she was right all along. Carrying these memories, the laughter, the tears, the friendships, was better than carrying regrets.

And maybe… that's the best way to end a chapter.

— Years That Slipped Away —

Final Board exams were finally over. The tension in the air had vanished. Everyone was breathing a little lighter, laughing louder, walking as if they had just dropped kilos of weight off their backs.

During exams, I spotted Gayatri a couple of times. She was there, head bent over books or question papers after exams. But we never made eye contact. Just a few months ago, we couldn't stop talking, and now… silence. Like two strangers standing at the same bus stop.

Then summer vacation arrived, and with it, life threw its own exam at me. My grandfather passed away. Our house was filled with relatives, rituals, and the heavy silence that comes after someone leaves. I remember Papa, sitting a little apart, lost in his thoughts. A week later, as if life was in a hurry to move on, Papa got a promotion. Along with it came a transfer to Mumbai.

It wasn't the usual, "Pack slowly, we'll shift after two months" kind of transfer. No. The earlier officer had died, so Papa had to take charge immediately. Within days, our bags were packed, cupboards emptied, and we were boarding a train. I didn't even get to say proper goodbyes to half my friends.

Results came soon after. I had managed 90%. Not bad, considering my habit of daydreaming during half the classes. Nidhi, of course, hit a rocket score, 98%. I later that Gayatri got 80%. A slip, but everyone knew why. Her mind had been elsewhere. Sometimes numbers don't tell the whole story.

And the LLB gang? Believe it or not, they passed. Nobody knows how. Maybe lady luck finally decided to sit with them in the exam hall.

Life in Mumbai was a new chapter altogether. The city didn't walk, it ran. Trains moved like snakes, honking cars became background music, and vada pav replaced samosas in my snack list. I joined college here, along with my CA course. Suddenly, days were longer, nights shorter, and sleep became a luxury.

By the end of college, I had managed to clear my CA. Honestly, that felt bigger than getting 90% in school. Later, I even cleared CFA. One exam after another, like climbing stairs in a building that had no lift. But each floor opened to a better view.

My professional journey began with a famous investment banking company. The office was all glass walls, suits, and people talking about millions as if they were thousands. I felt like a small-town boy trying to fit in among all the suits. But slowly, I found my place.

A couple of years later, marriage entered the scene. New chapter, new responsibilities, new kinds of happiness. Life rolled on, fast but steady. Promotions came, and one fine day, another transfer letter arrived. This time not to Mumbai or Delhi, but all the way to Sydney, Australia.

Standing there with that letter, I smiled. From scribbling on my hand during exams to getting a job in another country, it felt unreal. But I knew everything was connected.

When I look out of my Sydney office window at the tall buildings and rushing traffic, I sometimes see flashes of the old classroom. The chalk dust, the last bench laughter, the nervous glances before exams. Life moved on, yes. But a part of me will always remain there, in Ahmedabad, in those school corridors, laughing with friends who thought passing itself was a miracle.

Life in Sydney was good. Both of us had steady jobs, a decent salary, and a comfortable life. Everything was perfect. But life has its own way of throwing surprises when you least expect them.

That 'Promise'

2011- Australia

It was one of those routine mornings in the office.

As usual I was busy typing some report when my phone buzzed.

Unknown number. Australia code.

"Spam," I muttered and ignored it.

But it rang again. And again. Whoever it was, they were stubborn. With a sigh, I picked up.

"Hello?"

A pause. Then a voice I could never mistake.

"Hello… is this Gopal's number?"

My hand froze. That voice… it couldn't be.

"…Gayatri?"

"Yes," she whispered. Trying to sound normal, but her voice was trembling like someone holding back an ocean.

I leaned back in my chair, the office screen now a blur. "Gayatri? After so many years? Where are you? What's going on?"

There was silence, then a choked sob.

"Gopal…" her voice broke. "I'm in Melbourne… I'm in hospital… I need you, Gopal. Please… come fast. I don't have much time."

Those words hit me like a bullet to the chest. *Don't have much time?*

"Wait, wait, wait," I fired questions like a machine gun. "You're in Melbourne? Since when? What hospital? What happened? What do you mean no time? Gayatri, speak clearly!"

She tried to hold her breath steady. “I know you have so many questions. But I can’t explain now… not on the phone. I’ll send you the hospital details. Just come soon.”

I gripped the phone tighter. “At least tell me what’s wrong. Are you....”

Her voice cracked again. “Please, Gopal. Trust me once. Just come.”

And before I could press further, the line went dead.

For a full minute, I just stared at the phone screen, the number from Australia glowing like it carried a curse. My chest felt heavy, my mind racing.

Melbourne. Hospital. Don’t have much time.

Within the next hour, I had booked the first available flight.

I went straight from the airport to the hospital.

Didn’t even notice the city.

All I could hear in my head was her voice. *“I don’t have much time.”*

When I reached the ICU corridor, my legs froze.

Through the glass, I saw her.

Gayatri.

The girl who once filled classrooms with chatter, who argued over samosa bills in the Samosa shop, who danced during cultural day practice without caring what anyone thought. Now lying there, bruised, bandaged, tubes all around, fighting for every breath.

For a few seconds, I couldn’t step in. My heart didn’t allow it.

And then I noticed. Next to her bed, a small cradle.

Inside, a baby girl slept. Tiny fingers curled into fists, breathing softly, as if the world outside didn’t exist.

Tears pressed at my eyes.

A nurse touched my shoulder. “You can go in now.”

I nodded and walked in. My footsteps felt too loud for that room.

Gayatri turned her head slowly. Her eyes met mine.

For a moment, we didn't speak. Just looked at each other, years melting, and the distance between us shrinking at the same time.

She tried to smile. Weak, but real. With her hand, she gestured me to sit.

I pulled the chair closer. My throat was dry. Words had deserted me.

"Gopal, you look the same" She tried to smile.

"Thank you for coming," she whispered. Her voice was barely above a breath.

"I knew… no matter what, you would come."

I clenched my jaw, still silent.

She looked at me, eyes wet. "You have questions. So many. And you deserve answers. All of them."

I tried to speak. "Gayatri… what is..." but my voice cracked halfway.

Her gaze shifted to the cradle. She said softly. "My daughter."

The baby stirred, let out a tiny sigh, and slept again.

My lips parted, but nothing came.

Gayatri's eyes returned to me. They weren't just tired they were full of apology. Heavy with regrets only she could carry.

"Gopal," she whispered, "I owe you the truth."

I leaned closer. My hands trembled, resting on my knees.

For years I had imagined meeting her again, a college reunion, an old friends' wedding, maybe even a random airport lobby.

But not like this. Not in an ICU, with machines beeping, and death sitting in the corner like an uninvited guest.

She held my hand, her grip weak but desperate.

"Please listen," she said. "Whatever strength I have left, I want to use it to tell you everything."

I swallowed hard and nodded.

The beeping of the monitor filled the silence. The cradle rocked gently.

She closed her eyes for a second, gathering strength, then spoke.

"After Class XII… you remember Kabir, right?"

I nodded stiffly. Of course, how could I forget.

"My relationship with him… it didn't survive. Petty fights, silly egos, stubbornness. By the time college started, we were like strangers. He walked his way, I walked mine. It was messy, but I wanted to start fresh. Somewhere far away from all the old faces, all the old stories."

She coughed lightly. I moved to adjust her pillow, but she waved her hand, as if to say *I'm fine.*

"In my second year, I met Ajay," she continued. "Tamil Brahmin boy. Quiet, intelligent, patient… the opposite of me in every way. Friendship turned into something more. You know how it is, Gopal. Small jokes become long walks, long walks become late-night phone calls. By the time we realised, we were in love."

Her eyes softened, remembering.

"But love doesn't feed families, right? We told our parents. My Punjabi parents said no. His Tamil Brahmin parents said no. No discussion, no compromise, just straight rejection. 'Not our culture, not our people, not our way.'" She gave a tired laugh. "We thought time would melt their anger. Instead, it froze harder."

I clenched my fists. I could already see where this was going.

"So, we ran away," she whispered. "We thought, *let's build our own world.* New city, new life. In 2004, we came to Melbourne. Two suitcases, two beating hearts, zero backup. We opened a small restaurant with some friends. It wasn't fancy, but we worked hard. Ajay in the kitchen, me at the front. Slowly, the place grew. Customers loved us. For a few years, life felt perfect. We had nothing, yet we had everything."

Her voice softened again. "In 2010, my daughter was born. My little sunshine. I stepped back from work, became a full-time mother. Ajay carried the restaurant on his shoulders. We thought, this is it, we've made it."

She paused. The beeping of the monitor filled the silence.

"But destiny… it has a strange sense of humour."

Her lips trembled.

"Our business partners, the very friends we trusted, committed fraud. They siphoned money from the accounts, took loans from banks in the company's name. And then… they vanished. Gone. Left the entire liability on us."

I leaned forward. "What? You...."

She cut me off with a weak nod. "Yes. Overnight, we were buried in debt. Banks hounded us. Creditors banged on the doors. We sold our bungalow, moved into a small rented house. Every money we had saved went to pay off loans. And still, it wasn't enough."

Her voice broke, but she pushed on. "We borrowed small loans just to keep the restaurant alive. But when you cut costs, quality suffers. When quality suffers, customers stop coming. Slowly, our sales dropped. Repayments became a nightmare. Each day was a battle."

She turned her face away, tears rolling down.

"And then… last week… the car accident."

The words hung in the air like shattered glass.

I didn't breathe.

"Ajay died instantly," she whispered. Her chest rose and fell with pain. "I survived. Barely. My daughter was in day care, thank God. She was safe."

She looked at the cradle, her eyes softening. The baby stirred and stretched her little arms, then fell back into peaceful sleep.

I felt a lump rise in my throat.

Gayatri's hand trembled as she reached for mine. I held it gently.

"Gopal," she said, voice cracking. "You can see the truth now. I don't have much time. The doctors told me straight. Days, maybe. I can feel it too. Every breath feels borrowed."

Her words sliced me open.

She went quiet for a moment, then whispered, "Even my parents… they won't see me. I tried calling them. They don't want to meet me. Not me, not my daughter. They cut me off completely."

She turned her face towards me. Her eyes were full of regret, guilt, helplessness.

"And there's more you need to know, Gopal. About us… about that time in school. About why I misunderstood you. About Kabir. About the picnic to Lonavala."

I stiffened. My chest tightened. After all these years, was the truth finally coming out?

Gayatri squeezed my hand weakly. "I owe you everything, Gopal. Today, before it's too late, I will tell you all."

Gayatri held my hand tighter, though her grip was weak. Her eyes searched mine, desperate, almost pleading.

"Gopal… after my breakup with Kabir, I carried a lot of anger. I blamed myself, I blamed him, and sometimes…" her voice trembled, "I even blamed you."

I looked at her, stunned. "Me? Why?"

She blinked away tears. "Because of what happened in Lonavala. That stupid picnic. You remember?"

My stomach twisted. *Lonavala.* That one weekend had haunted me for years.

She continued, "After the breakup, Dinesh from Kabir's class... he came to me. He told me everything. The truth. That it was Kabir who had asked him to lie. To create distance between us. Kabir didn't like our friendship, Gopal. He thought you were the wall between me and him. So, he poisoned everything. I trusted his version. I doubted you."

Her voice cracked. "And that was my biggest mistake. I misjudged you. I doubted the one friend who always stood by me."

I sat frozen. So many years, so much pain, all because of a lie.

"Gayatri..." I whispered, "Why didn't you tell me earlier? Why now?"

She shook her head. "When I moved to Melbourne, I knew you were in Sydney. I had your number from the school group. So many times, I typed it... stared at it... but I couldn't dial. I didn't have the courage. How could I face you, after what I had done?"

Her tears fell freely now. "I kept waiting for the right moment. I thought maybe someday, at a reunion, or a wedding... we'd laugh about the past, and I'd finally tell you. But not like this. Never like this."

The room felt smaller, air heavier. I looked at the cradle again. Little princess slept peacefully, her tiny chest rising and falling, unaware that her world was about to change forever.

Gayatri followed my gaze. Her voice softened. "Gopal... she's all I have. All I leave behind. And she has no one else."

I swallowed hard, my throat dry.

She took a long breath. "Even my parents have turned their back. Ajay's family never forgave him. Everyone abandoned us." She looked at me with trembling eyes. "You are the only person I trust."

I shook my head, overwhelmed. "Gayatri... don't say that. You'll recover. We'll fight this. Doctors are wrong sometimes....."

She squeezed my hand weakly. "No, Gopal. Don't lie to yourself. I feel it. My body knows. I don't have much time."

Silence pressed between us, broken only by the monitor's beep.

Then, with all the strength she had left, she whispered, "Promise me."

I looked at her, confused. "Promise what?"

Her eyes flicked towards the cradle. "Promise me you'll take care of my daughter. Please."

I froze. The weight of her words crushed me. This wasn't a small favour. This was a life. A child's future. A promise that would rewrite my own life.

My mouth went dry. "Gayatri… this is……"

"Please," she cut in, desperate. "I know it's too much. I know I don't deserve to ask. But I have no one else. If I close my eyes knowing my daughter has you, I can go in peace."

I looked at her. The girl who once laughed without fear, who once fought with me over silly things, who once stopped talking to me because of a lie… now lying broken before me, begging me to take care of the most precious piece of her life.

My heart ached. Tears blurred my vision.

I leaned closer, held her hand firmly, and whispered, "I promise."

Her eyes closed, tears slipping out. Relief washed over her face. "Thank you," she whispered, almost inaudible. "I knew… you would never let me down."

The cradle rocked gently, almost as if she had heard the promise too. The beeping of the monitor kept time with my heartbeat, heavy and unsteady.

I sat there, holding Gayatri's hand, knowing I had just made the heaviest promise of my life.

Year 2020

By 2020, life had shifted into a new routine. Office, home, the usual grind. Things weren't perfect, but they were steady.

Then came another phone call that shook me. This time, from India.

It was my mother. Her voice was trembling. My father had suffered a massive heart attack. Doctors managed to save him, but the damage was done. He was weak now, dependent on someone to be around him all the time.

The words hit me hard. My parents had retired a few years back and were living peacefully in Ahmedabad. They had refused to come with me to Australia. "We want to spend our last years close to our relatives, our temples, our city," my father always said.

For them, home was not about comfort. It was about belonging.

Now, with his health broken, they needed me.

I sat that evening in silence. Life in Australia had given me stability, a career, a routine I could manage with my eyes closed. But roots are stronger than routines. And in that moment, I knew where I had to be.

The decision was not easy, but it was simple. I would move to Ahmedabad.

Luckily, my company was already planning to open an Asia regional office there. I requested to lead it, and after a few weeks of back-and-forth, the approval came through. Sometimes life shows you a path when you least expect it.

Leaving Australia was not easy. Packing up felt like closing a chapter I never imagined ending. Years of life reduced to cartons, luggage, and checklists. On the flight, as the lights dimmed, I kept thinking of my father waiting for me, weaker than I had ever seen him.

Ahmedabad welcomed me with its heat, its chaos, and its warmth. The city was noisy, crowded, unpredictable, but it wrapped around me like a long-lost relative. Relatives and neighbours filled the house with food, advice, and endless questions. My mother cried every time she saw me, as if afraid I would vanish again. My father, thinner and more fragile than ever, held my hand and whispered, "Now the home is complete."

Life in Ahmedabad was not new to me. I had grown up in these lanes, seen these markets, prayed in these temples. Nothing here surprised me, not even the traffic that still refused to follow rules, relatives still arrived without notice, and neighbours still believed every house on the street was one big family.

But this time, it felt different. Earlier, I had wanted to run away from all this, chase something bigger. Now, I found comfort in the same noise I once escaped.

Office in the day, family in the evening, temple bells echoing at night, everything carried a rhythm I already knew.

Of course, there were challenges. Managing an ageing father's health, balancing office demands with constant relatives, sitting through endless conversations where everyone wanted to advise me on life, none of it was easy. But beneath all of it was a calm I had never felt before.

This city wasn't giving me anything new. It was just giving me back everything I had forgotten to value. And in that return, I felt something I hadn't felt in years, that I was finally where I was meant to be.

And in that chaos, I realised something. Life doesn't always give us what we plan. It just keeps moving, asking us to show up where we are needed most.

2025- Present day

It was Sara's birthday.

The house was buzzing that evening. Laughter, music, balloons tied at every corner.

I stood at my bedroom door, watching her from a distance. She was in the middle of the hall, cracking jokes, pulling faces, making everyone laugh. The same spark, the same fire.

My eyes softened. For a moment, the noise around me faded. All I could see was her, running around, owning the room like she had been born to shine.

"They were right," I thought, "she didn't get my DNA. She got something better, her mother's spirit… and my promise."

No, she didn't have my quiet nature. She had Gayatri's fire.

And that was perfect.

A voice broke my thoughts.

"Gopal, what are you doing here? LLB gang is here… come fast," my wife called from the hallway.

I smiled faintly. "Oh, they came? Okay, you take care of them, I'm coming in two minutes."

She turned to go, then paused when I said softly, "By the way, Nidhi…"

She looked back. "Hmm?"

"Thanks. For everything. For all your support in life."

She paused looking at the wooden box, then smiled gently. "I understand your emotions but stop being filmy and come out fast." And she walked away.

I put all those memories back in the box… and kept it in the cupboard. Safe. Untouched.

Some stories are not meant to be forgotten. They are just meant to be kept carefully.

I stood up, took a deep breath, and stepped out.

I turned back towards the hall. The LLB gang was already shouting, pulling each other's legs like the old days. But my eyes stayed on Sara.

Fifteen years since that day in Melbourne. Since Gayatri's trembling voice on the phone. Since her weak hand in mine, asking me for the hardest promise of my life.

That night, in that ICU, I had whispered, *"I promise."*

And today, standing here, I knew I had kept it.

Sara had grown, not just into a daughter, but into a bridge between past and present. Every smile of hers carried Gayatri's laughter. Every stubborn fight carried Gayatri's fire. Every small kindness reminded me of the girl who once filled classrooms with chatter and courage.

I took a deep breath.

The party was loud, but inside me, there was a calm. A calm that comes when you know a circle has completed itself.

I closed my eyes and whispered silently, "Gayatri, you don't have to worry. Your daughter is fine. She's happy. She's loved. And I kept my promise."

A balloon burst in the hall, kids screamed and laughed. Sara turned for a second, caught my eye, and waved. I waved back.

For her, it was just a birthday.

For me, it was the proof of a promise.

And maybe that's what life really is.

Not perfect stories. Not grand endings. Just promises we try our best to keep.

-------------- *That's how it was: Those days…that promise* --------------